"This book is filled with stress-reducing tools that effectively guide readers down a path leading to increased self-awareness, authenticity, personal power, and fulfillment. Trina shares her insightful wisdom through poignant examples and easy-to-follow exercises. I highly recommend this comprehensive book."

—**Naras Bhat, M.D., F.A.C.P.**
Author of *Reversing Stress and Burnout*

"In the flood of recent self-help books, Trina Swerdlow's *Stress Reduction Journal* emerges as a jewel. Its straightforward, practical, and user-friendly style provides all the tools every stressed-out person desperately needs."

—**Loren E. Pedersen, Ph.D.**
Jungian psychoanalyst and author of *Dark Hearts: The Unconscious Forces That Shape Men's Lives, Sixteen Men: Understanding Masculine Personality Types,* and *The Soul Grows in Darkness.*

"In a powerful testimonial to her authenticity, Trina Swerdlow has combined what she has learned through her own personal life challenges with a lifelong commitment to helping others. In *Stress Reduction Journal* she provides tools to help us explore who we are—physically, mentally, emotionally, and spiritually. This wonderful resource can empower us to own both our power and vulnerabilities, thereby claiming our own authenticity."

—**Len Saputo, M.D.**
Founder and Director of the Health Medicine Forum and Health Medicine Institute in Lafayette, California

Stress Reduction Journal

Stress Reduction Journal

Meditate and Journal Your Way to Better Health

Trina Swerdlow, C.C.H.T.

iUniverse, Inc.
New York Lincoln Shanghai

Stress Reduction Journal
Meditate and Journal Your Way to Better Health

iUniverse books may be ordered through booksellers or by contacting:

iUniverse
2021 Pine Lake Road, Suite 100
Lincoln, NE 68512
www.iuniverse.com
1-800-Authors (1-800-288-4677)

ISBN-13: 978-0-595-37455-7 (pbk)
ISBN-13: 978-0-595-81849-5 (ebk)
ISBN-10: 0-595-37455-7 (pbk)
ISBN-10: 0-595-81849-8 (ebk)

Printed in the United States of America

I dedicate this book
to my inspiring clients,
who courageously explore
and water
their inner landscapes—
to experience
the sacred home
within themselves.

Contents

Acknowledgments

I want to express gratitude to the following people
who have touched my life in memorable ways.
Some folks listed here have a direct connection
to the birth of this book, while others
simply nourish my soul.

First of all, Grandma Rose, thank you for being a source of light in my childhood when the darkness felt overwhelming—your unconditional love was a gift to my hungry heart. Gloria Dunn-Violin, you're a dear friend and *inspiring Power Partner*—the ongoing loving support between us is priceless! Neal Sideman, you're brilliant and I am blessed by our precious connection. Judy Phillips, I treasure all the synchronistic moments we've shared through the thick and thin of the growth process—our friendship will forever be poetry-in-motion. Karen Carbone and Tracey Prever you are my Spiritual Sisters. Deep appreciation to Michelle Larson-Speir for many years of friendship and for sharing your wonderful family with me; Matthew, Emily, and Chuck. Janet Lee Taylor Velasco, Glo Reese, Susan Miller, Rona Jackson, Sue Gannon, Margaret Bafalon, Karen Shertzer, and Madeline Mischo Shelby—I am delighted our heartfelt paths crossed. Richard Carlson, you are an amazing person—your continual enthusiasm for my writing and art is received with sincere gratitude. Loren Pedersen, I appreciate your keen "editor's eye" and the relentless support we share for one another's dreams. Peter W. Hagen, you did an excellent job as an additional editor of this book. Christy Kaplan, thank you for driving to my office in the pouring rain and then inviting me to teach at the Women's Health Center—your passion for helping others is truly admirable. Finally, Holly Holmes-Meredith, your hypnotherapy training was personally and professionally transformational—*thank you from the bottom of my heart.*

My life and love of writing are enriched
by knowing each of you.

To protect individual privacy, all names and identifying details of clients and others cited in this book have been changed. The final examples are therefore fictional. I hope the examples shared will serve as inspiring mirrors for personal growth.

Introduction

The numerous benefits I have received from meditating and journaling over the last twenty-five years inspired me to write this book. Unfortunately, I know stress way too well. I know both *subtle* levels of stress, as well as *acute* levels of stress. My expertise is not simply because in 1989 I wrote *Growing Free;* a book about anxiety, or worked on *Reversing Stress and Burnout* with Naras Bhat, M.D. from 2000 to 2002, or because I'm a Certified Clinical Hypnotherapist.

My personal experience with stress comes from being a trauma survivor of a severely abusive childhood. As a result, my adrenal glands learned from an early age to be on *red alert.* Stress has been both a thorn in my side, and a *profound teacher* for me. Thank God for the latter. I've learned a great deal about compassion and self-love from having such an intimate and ongoing relationship with trauma-related stress.

Over the years, I have worked with numerous stress-reduction tools. In addition to using existing tools, I have created many of my own. In this book, I will share what has been most effective for me and for my clients. If you are also a trauma survivor, I highly recommend that you work with a qualified therapist while you explore any tools in this book. In addition to my input, you deserve experienced guidance and support.

The Stress-Management Tools you will learn through various exercises in this book address the mind, body, and spirit. This practical philosophy of stress management works from the *inside out.* In addition, it's wise to assess what *outer changes* in your life could *decrease* your stress. Then, make as many of those healthy outer changes as you can. By doing so, you will be stress-busting internally as well as externally—thus creating a *full-spectrum approach!*

The sparkling gem featured on this book's cover is a symbol for the full-spectrum philosophy. The colorful gem illustrates the *Inner Light* that shines as a result of exploring, refining, and polishing various facets of yourself. Facets may include your inborn talents, communication style, emotions, habits, intuition, and self-esteem.

The meditation and journaling exercises in this book will assist you to explore and integrate many of your colorful facets. This process can lead to increased internal congruency and heighten your ability to live from an authentic place. Authenticity is about *being real* and owning *your power,* as well as, *your vulnerability.* Numerous clients who come to see me for stress-related issues are either over-identified with their *power* or over-identified with their *vulnerability.*

For example, I have seen new clients who initially had little or no connection to their emotional vulnerabilities. However, their bodies were expressing their vulnerabilities through stress-related symptoms. The symptoms were desperately trying to get their attention and, *when they got loud enough*, the wake-up calls were finally heard. Often, once the emotional issues were addressed and new tools were utilized, the stress-related symptoms subsided.

I have also worked with many would-be "Superwomen" who were *disconnected* from their emotional vulnerabilities. These bright women were often working professionals, wives, and mothers who continually gave to others but received little nurturing in return. When their vulnerabilities *finally* surfaced, sometimes due to exhaustion, few people in their lives knew how to deal with them. The balancing work for these women was to begin *integrating their vulnerabilities* into the previous sense they had of themselves as being all-powerful. They grew first by finding out what their needs were. Then, they began teaching their loved ones how to meet those needs.

Also, I have seen stressed clients who, because of their wounding in childhood, became over-identified with their *vulnerabilities*. Part of our work together was tapping into their disowned power so that their power could be integrated into their identities. When these clients had some *internal power* in place, they became better equipped to pursue their goals and create fulfilling lives. In addition, through this balancing process, they cultivated stronger abilities to self-soothe the vulnerabilities from their early wounds. As a result, they increased their *overall resilience and personal power.*

Feelings: Important Messengers

When we are stressed by the demands of life, it is easy to look for ways to distract ourselves from the feelings that are stirring within us. Instead of seeing our feelings as *allies* that have important messages for us, many of us see them as *enemies* that need to be avoided. That is when we go into a *flight mode* away from our feelings. For some people, the avoidance of feelings works for a while.

However, for most of us, the feelings sooner or later begin to leak out—*and it isn't always pretty.* The unconscious *leakage of feelings* can manifest through:

- Our Behaviors
- Our Bodily Symptoms
- Other People's Behaviors

Our Behaviors

Imagine we are driving through our lives in *psychological cars.** Let's say that we don't know how to deal directly with our angry feelings, so we hide them in the *trunks* of our cars. After awhile, the intensity of those feelings begins to build. As a result of the pressure, our cars' trunks pop open uncontrollably on a regular basis and we spew anger. In these times, we may find ourselves forgetting important commitments and arguing with others. We may explode over *little things* that aren't at all related to what we're *really* angry about.

As a result, feelings that are not addressed may unconsciously be *expressed* through our behaviors. One indication that our car trunks have popped open is our startle responses to the intensity of the feelings that "snuck out." We may shockingly ask ourselves, "Where in the world did *that* come from?" If we want to avoid ownership of the feelings and subsequent behaviors, we may tell ourselves that they came *out of the blue.* However, *out of our trunks* is often a more realistic description.

Our Bodily Symptoms

After years of depositing angry feelings into our trunks, can you imagine how *heavy* the back ends of our cars would become? Eventually, the front wheels would be lifted up off the ground—we could call this motion an *anger wheelie!* Think about how stressful that overloaded trunk's weight would be on the back tires. If the pressure wasn't released, one or both tires could easily blow out at any time.

---

*The "psychological car" concept comes from *Embracing Our Selves,* by Hal and Sidra Stone.

Unfortunately, I can relate to this example. For the first twenty-plus years of my life, I had irritable bowel problems. I had suppressed lots of emotions from my painful childhood. My poor intestinal tract struggled to hold the suppressed fear and anger that were buried deep inside of me (or the trunk of my psychological car).

The good news is, when I dealt with my suppressed feelings through therapy, my intestinal problems miraculously disappeared. Thank God—I haven't needed Pepto-Bismol in the *gallon jug* for the past twenty years!

Other People's Behaviors

In *What You Feel, You Can Heal,* best-selling author John Gray says that *what we suppress, others may express.* He explains that if we are suppressing strong emotions, then someone else in our household may end up expressing our buried feelings. As a result, our partners, kids, or pets may unconsciously act out our suppressed emotional material.

For example, Joel was in his third marriage when he came to me for hypnotherapy. Joel's medical doctor recommended he learn some stress management techniques due to the chronic health challenges he was having. Joel blamed all of his stress on his current marital problems. He claimed his wife, Helen, was an emotional mess. He said, "She's so irrational, emotional, and frankly—she's *hysterical* most of the time!" Joel clarified how all of his wives were independent and rational women when he first fell in love with them. He said, "But, after a year or so of marriage, they each became *an emotional basket case.* Why am I destined to put up with these *hysterical types?*"

Through our work, Joel realized that he was following the unconscious conditioning from his childhood to *avoid his vulnerability.* He had been stuffing his fearful feelings into the trunk of his psychological car since he was a young boy. As a result, his wives ended up expressing their own as well as *his suppressed fear* (and his other unexpressed vulnerable feelings). Consequently, it was no wonder that each of Joel's wives ended up feeling *overwhelmed* with vulnerability.

Another example was my client Victoria, who at forty sought hypnotherapy for weight loss. Shortly into our work it became apparent that Victoria followed the unconscious conditioning from her family and from societal influences—*not to express anger.* In childhood, she remembered hearing her parents say, "Girls should be seen and not heard."

From our work together, Victoria discovered that unaddressed hostility and sadness were *weighing down* the trunk of her psychological car. These painful feelings had been accumulating since she was a little girl. Thus, her husband Brad was unconsciously working overtime when it came to anger expression, unfortunately, *enough for the two of them.* Although he was never physically violent, Brad's anger was being expressed verbally through emotional outbursts. When Victoria learned healthy ways to deal with her anger, her weight began to drop and her marriage stabilized—*along with Brad's anger.*

So keep in mind that *what we suppress, others may express* is reversible. It can become—*what others suppress, we may express.* The distortion of feelings can happen in either direction. Can you see how feelings are *important messengers* that need to be clearly understood and addressed? And of course, even if there's suppression and the resulting expression dynamics in a relationship, the bottom line is—everyone needs to accept *full responsibility* for his or her own feelings and behaviors.

The meditation and journaling exercises in this book were designed to assist you in making your feelings *allies* rather than *nuisances* or *enemies.* Through working with this material, you will be less likely to have your behaviors, bodily symptoms, or other people's behaviors unconsciously affect your health and well-being. When you embrace the messages that your feelings offer, instead of avoiding them, you will have an opportunity to become *deeply acquainted with yourself.* Thus, you gain the *valuable wisdom* that your emotions carry.

Full Spectrum Stress-Management Tools

Each chapter of this book offers information on a particular topic. After reading the topic discussion, you will have an opportunity to explore the Stress-Management Tool for that chapter. By completing a few simple exercises that include both meditation and journaling, you can experience the tool *in action.* Keep in mind that the Stress-Management Tools offered here are *not* substitutes for traditional medical care, but they can complement working with a practitioner in the healing arts.

Working with these tools will assist you in countering your *Stress Responses* and inviting in *Relaxation Responses.* A *Stress Response* is the result of an increase in arousal of both the body and the mind. A *Relaxation Response* is the result of letting go at both the body and the mind levels. By following the full-spectrum approach to stress management in this book, you will learn to lessen stress by strengthening your capabilities in the following personal growth areas:

- Emotional Intelligence (E.Q.)
  Reduce stress by identifying how you're feeling and where you're holding tension in your body.

- Communication Skills
  Learn the art of listening and how to recognize unhealthy communication dynamics.

- Behavioral Health
  Trace habits down to their sources to interrupt behaviors that are unhealthy and learn to make healthier choices.

- Transitions & Change
  Heighten your perspective while navigating the uncertainty of change.

- Intuition
  Tap into your *inner wisdom* for guidance.

- Self-esteem
  Increase your ability to see yourself through soft, loving, and compassionate eyes.

- Soulful Exploration
  Discover ways to nourish yourself through activities that feed your soul.

After working with these important topics, you will have a number of tools to manage your stress more effectively. As a result, you will optimize your overall health and well-being. Now if you're ready for some exciting scientific documentation to further inspire you to begin meditating and journaling—*read on!*

Benefits of Meditating and Journaling

Over the last thirty years, more than one thousand studies exploring the effects of meditation have been reported in scientific publications. Brain scans, EEGs, and blood tests are only some of the scientific research methods used. These studies provide concrete evidence of *physical and psychological benefits* of meditation.

In the stillness of meditation, we calm the tensions of our minds and bodies by learning how to *let go*. Physical benefits of meditating include increased stamina and energy, faster recovery, significantly lowered blood pressure, and reductions in stress-related diseases such as heart disease and hypertension. Meditation also significantly lowers physical pain from back injury and arthritis. In addition, meditation improves coordination, motor skills, and sports performance.

Several hundred studies confirm that a daily *twenty-minute meditation practice* improves one's psychological state and maximizes the ability to perform mentally. Other benefits include: decreased anxiety and depression, as well as increased concentration, empathy, and creativity.

Journaling is also scientifically shown to lower stress and improve health. By putting pen-to-paper, we consciously *externalize* our thoughts and feelings to explore what is going on in our internal landscapes. The stress release comes when we embrace and then let go of our frustrations and worries. As a result, we are not keeping our stresses pent-up and internalized—they come out into the light of day to be recognized, processed, *and then released*.

So, if you are ready to meditate and journal your way to better health, then simply turn the page and step onto this stress-management path. Isn't it time to slow down and *come home to yourself*?

Beginner's Simple Meditation

Sitting in meditation is a wonderful way to begin your day by *going inward before going outward.* Morning meditation creates a gentle transition or bridge from your deep nightly sleep to a waking state. If you choose, you can let a peaceful meditation *welcome you* into each day.

Meditation is an opportunity to bring your mind-body awareness into the *present moment.* However, this is sometimes easier said than done. During meditation, you may find yourself thinking about the past or the future. Don't fret; it is common for people who are new to meditation to have *busy minds.* For this reason, using a *mantra* to give the mind a reference point can be helpful to new meditators. A mantra is the silent (or quiet) repetition of a sound or word during meditation. *One, ah-h-h, home, shalom,* or *om-m-m* are examples of different mantras.

To encourage patience, meditation teachers often share the following analogy with their students:

♦ ♦

> Learning to quiet the mind is like paper-training a puppy. When the puppy wanders off the paper to relieve itself, you don't shame it. You simply notice that it has left the paper and then you gently coax the puppy back. Similarly, notice when your mind has left the mantra and gently coax it back. Given that having a wandering mind during meditation is normal, there is no need to judge or shame yourself.

♦ ♦

For example, while meditating, if you find yourself thinking about where you are going to have lunch, simply notice that you are thinking about the *future.* You might say to yourself, "Oh, future thinking." Then, coax your mind back to the *present moment* by repeating the mantra. If you notice that you are thinking about the *past,* then you might say to yourself, "Oh, past thinking." Then, coax your mind back to the present moment again by repeating the mantra.

Be aware that, at first, the mind may resist quieting down and meditating. However, like the puppy analogy, with patience many people can train their minds to return to the present moment by using the mantra. Patience is the key. The benefits of meditation result from interrupting habitual thinking, quieting the mind-body, and learning how to be in the *present moment.*

You may want to do the Beginner's Simple Meditation, each morning, and then read a chapter from this book each evening. At the end of each chapter, you will find exercises that include a short meditation and some journaling. The meditation exercises focus on a topic, and they don't use a mantra as this Beginner's Simple Meditation does. Therefore, you will have an opportunity to practice two styles of meditation while using this book. They are:

- The Beginner's Simple Meditation practice (with a mantra)
- Topic oriented meditation exercises at the end of each chapter (no mantra)

Preparing for the Simple Beginner's Meditation

Now it is time to explore some basics: when, where, and how long to meditate. Once you have digested this information, you can explore what mantra you would like to use during the Simple Beginner's Meditation.

When?

Think about *when* you would like to fit a regular meditation practice into your schedule. Keep in mind that it is advisable to meditate before meals or after fully digesting your meal. Meditating before breakfast, before dinner, or at bedtime are ideal times to consider. A good foundation for reducing and managing your stress is to establish *regularity and structure* for your meditation practice.

Where?

To prepare for meditation, think about *where* you are going to meditate. Have a watch or clock accessible. If you plan to meditate at home, then choose a consistent place. Hang a "*Meditating, Do Not Disturb*" sign on your door if you need to let family members know when you are meditating. Keep in mind that by setting your boundaries clearly, you will be modeling good *self-care.*

Of course, never meditate when you need to be aware of your surroundings. For example, don't meditate if you are alone in a park. Moreover, never meditate while operating a motor vehicle or equipment of any kind. If possible, turn off pagers and let voice mail automatically take messages for you. This is your time to relax, let go, and recharge!

How Long?

Think about *how long* you would like to spend during each of your meditation sessions. Meditating for as little as *ten minutes* a day has been shown to provide positive results in managing stress. In addition, if you want to receive maximal benefits from meditating, then *twenty minutes, twice a day* is an ideal commitment. If *fifteen minutes* once or twice a day feels right to you, then go with that. You can always add additional time later.

If you haven't meditated before, then start meditating in small increments. Gradually build up to the time that you desire. For the first week, meditate five to eight minutes only. Then, slowly *increase your time meditating* each week by five-minute increments until you are up to whatever time you chose as your goal. Ease into your mediation practice; there is *no rush.*

Say What?

Decide which *mantra* you would like to *say* during your meditations. "*Ah-h-h…*" *is* the one I teach new clients. However, if you test-drive "*ah-h-h…*" *and* it doesn't feel right, then consider one of the following words or sounds instead: *home, shalom, calm, peace, one, om-m-m, now…*When you effortlessly repeat the mantra through your natural exhalation, it can create the same relaxing effect as hearing the sounds of a stream or the ocean. For best results, consistently use whatever mantra you choose. That way, you will strengthen the association of *relaxation and calmness* with the sound of your mantra.

Beginner's Simple Meditation in Five Steps

Now that you have completed your preparation, follow these simple steps to go inward and connect with your inner landscape through meditation.

♦♦♦♦♦♦♦♦♦♦♦♦♦♦♦♦♦♦♦♦♦♦♦♦

1. Choose a place to sit

Meditating is a personal experience that should honor your needs. With this in mind, choose a place to sit that will allow you to be comfortable during your meditation time. You can sit on a chair or on the floor, whichever place is most comfortable for you. However, lying down may encourage falling asleep, so try sitting while meditating.

If you decide to sit on a chair, choose one that supports your lower back. Allow your feet to connect with the floor and rest your hands in your lap. Keep your head up, your back straight, and your shoulders relaxed. If possible, sit in the same place each time you meditate. Consistently doing so will encourage you to *relax automatically* whenever you return to your designated meditation place.

2. Close your eyes

If your eyes flutter or open after you close them, then gently close them again without squeezing them tightly shut.

3. Observe your breath

Initially, monitor your breathing with your hands. For example, put one hand on your upper chest and the other hand on your belly. Without judgment, observe your breathing for a minute or two. As you breathe, notice which one of your hands is moving, or are both of your hands moving? The goal is to breathe from your belly. Therefore, the hand on your belly should be the only one moving. Observe your breathing for a minute or two and then relax your hands into your lap. After you have been meditating regularly and are consistently breathing from your belly, then feel free to skip the hand monitoring part of this step. At that point, simply observe your belly breathing for a minute or two.

4. Repeat your mantra

If your environment permits, begin saying your mantra out loud. For a few minutes quietly say, "*Ah-h-h...*" (or whatever mantra you have chosen) throughout your exhalation. Sit silently as you inhale each time. After a few minutes of saying your mantra out loud, let the mantra become quieter until eventually there is no outer sound at all. Then, silently imagine hearing your mantra repeating in your mind.

If saying your mantra aloud is not appropriate for your environment, then begin by imagining that you are hearing it silently. Either way, simply let your belly breathing and your mantra lead you to a quiet place inside yourself—*home to your inner landscape.*

When your mind wanders, then gently bring your awareness back to the *present moment* and continue repeating the mantra. Try not to worry whether you are meditating "correctly." Cultivating a compassionate attitude toward yourself while meditating is highly recommended.

5. Return

After your allotted time is up, gently bring your awareness back to where you are and open your eyes. Take your time returning to an active state.

♦♦♦♦♦♦♦♦♦♦♦♦♦♦♦♦♦♦♦♦♦♦♦♦

So there you have the Beginner's Simple Meditation in five easy steps. The eventual goal is to connect with your *calm and peaceful* inner landscape whenever you have the need. For example, when you are feeling upset or stressed, you can tap into the peacefulness inside yourself that you have cultivated during your meditations. Your inner landscape will become easier to access after it has been *watered and nourished on a regular basis.*

Troubleshooting: Common Obstacles for Meditators

Often there are two common obstacles or distractions that a new meditator experiences: a busy mind and an agitated body. Let's discuss the mind aspect first. A busy mind may express itself, as mentioned earlier, by thinking about the past or the future. I often hear clients complain that they have too much chatter in their heads during meditation. I call this annoying distraction *brain chatter.* For example, brain chatter occurs when we are trying to meditate or sleep—but our minds are still active. In these outwardly quiet times, we have an opportunity to hear the chatter from the *cast of characters* inside our heads.

As a meditator for more than twenty years, I have certainly experienced my share of resistance from various inner characters during my meditation practices. Yep, I have become intimately acquainted with my own colorful cast that often expresses when I first sit down to meditate. In addition to my crew, I have had numerous opportunities to hear about my meditation students' inner characters as well. As a result, I have identified some archetypal *key players* who are experts at interrupting a peaceful meditation.

For example, the Inner Pusher is one of the most common characters known to chatter during meditation. The Inner Pusher is the goal-oriented part of a person who thrives on making numerous to-do lists. This pushy part has difficulty relaxing—especially if there remains a task or two on the *never-ending list.* And as my grandma used to say, "Heaven forbid there should be unfinished business at the end of the day!" Let's face it, people are multifaceted and complex. Within each of us are various aspects or characters who sometimes get into power struggles with one another.

Therefore, if you have a strong conviction to practice meditation regularly, then you might want to prepare yourself for some inner resistance. Below is a compilation of various inner characters and examples of their satirical comments during meditation. You may recognize this chatter from a few of these folks in your next meditation.

Six Internal Characters & Their Commentary During Meditation

1. **Pusher/Doer:** *"As soon as this twenty minutes is up I'm going to mow the lawn, wash the car, pick up the dry cleaning, walk the dog..."*
2. **Rebel:** *"This is ridiculous—I could've slept in!"*
3. **Worrier:** *"What if I miss an important phone call while I'm meditating?! Should I get up and answer it if the phone rings—or just sit here missing a once-in-a-lifetime opportunity?"*
4. **Inner Critic:** *"If you were more disciplined you would meditate four times a day, seven days a week, AND your posture would be exactly 90 degrees in relation to the floor. Face it—you're a bona fide spiritual flop."*

5. **Caregiver:** *"If I were really a good friend, I would be calling to check on Caroline—instead of sitting here doing nothing. She was so depressed yesterday. I should be cheering her up right now."*

6. **Antsy Inner Child:** *"Are we there yet?"*

Do any of these inner voices sound familiar? As discussed earlier with the puppy paper-training analogy, try to be nonjudgmental while observing your various inner characters and their chatter.* Simply notice and acknowledge, "Oh, there's my Inner Pusher revving to go. And, I'm choosing to take this time to meditate—the chores will wait." Then coax your mind back to the present moment by repeating the mantra.

Feeling physically agitated is another common distraction that may come up during meditation. You might feel an itch somewhere or experience discomfort in some part of your body. Unless the physical sensation is an ache or pain that you need to attend to, then simply acknowledge it. For example, if your nose is itching, you may want to scratch it once and then if it feels like a recurring distraction, you might say to yourself, "Oh, my nose feels itchy. And, I'm going to return my focus back to my mantra now." If agitation seems excessive, physical exercise or practicing yoga prior to meditating can be helpful.

The good news is that meditation is an invitation for all of us to slow down and gently move past our distractions. By breaking the cycle of a continual *doing mode*—each of us can gently relax into a *being mode* that honors the sacredness of the *present moment.* Finally, this quiet place gives us an opportunity to reduce our stress levels while becoming more deeply acquainted with ourselves. What a healthy gift we give our minds and bodies each time we meditate by *going inward before going outward.*

---

*If you would like to explore your inner characters further, consider reading *Embracing Our Selves,* by Hal and Sidra Stone.

How to Journal

Journaling is the act of putting *pen to paper* and giving your inner landscape *a voice.* Your writing voice can help you access whatever is quietly *(or noisily)* stirring in your gut. Journaling is an invitation to move below the surface of your exterior—beyond your name, gender, profession, degrees, and titles. When your innermost thoughts and feelings take form through the written word you are invited to ask and discover, "Who am I and how am I feeling—*really?*"

Writing freely, without worrying about spelling, grammar, or punctuation, can be a direct line to your *juice-filled essence.* For this reason, giving yourself permission to emote on paper can be good for your soul! In addition, journaling can serve as a tool that will assist you in making friends with your worries. For example, journaling before going to sleep will affirm your thoughts and feelings, thus encouraging you to experience a more *restful sleep.*

Here are four simple steps to prepare you for journaling:

1. Think about when you would like to fit regular journaling sessions into your schedule. Some people enjoy meditating in the morning and journaling afterward. Other folks like to meditate in the morning and journal every evening before going to sleep. There are no rules about when to journal. However, keep in mind that *regularity and structure* can be good for reducing and managing stress. In addition to your scheduled journaling times, spontaneously journaling when needed can be effective. For instance, if you wake up in the middle of the night and can't go back to sleep, consider journaling to *give voice* to whatever is bothering you.

2. Now let's talk about privacy. Since you will want to express freely in your journal, think about how to *ensure your privacy.* If you are not certain that others in your household will respect the privacy of your journal, then you can talk with them. Ask for each person's commitment to honor your boundaries. Another option is to store your journal in a lockable file cabinet of which you are the only key holder. Creating a safe container for your journaling process will assist you in reducing stress. On the other hand, you will be adding to your stress if you are worrying about whether your personal entries may be read by another. For this reason, ensuring your privacy is an important part of becoming a consistent and relaxed journal-keeper.

3. Although there are designated pages for journaling throughout this book, some people prefer to write in a separate, blank journal. Simple spiral-bound,

blank journals or spiral notebooks with lined pages lend themselves by staying fully open and flat during the writing process. Think about which option fits your needs.

4. Keep a pen or pencil with your journal so that you can easily begin writing whenever the urge strikes. If you are open to doodling in your journal, you may also want some colored pens or pencils easily accessible.

So now you have the basics for journaling:

- When you would like to journal
- How to ensure your personal privacy
- What you are going to journal in
- What writing tools appeal to you

After you have addressed these four issues and have your *tools in hand,* turn to the first chapter. Get ready to do some major stress reduction by taming saber-toothed tigers. Know that wearing a safari hat while working with the first chapter is *totally optional.*

At the end of every chapter, you will receive simple instructions for meditating and journaling. Following the instructions will decrease your stress levels and increase your self-awareness. Finally, keep in mind that expressing your inner landscape through journaling gives you an opportunity to discover buried treasures—*hopefully a trunk full of gems!*

1

Tiger Taming

The wind howls through the dense foliage in a prehistoric jungle. It is a dark landscape filled with hundreds of hungry predators and their prey. Night after night, the *survival-of-the-fittest cycle* continually plays out. The stronger creatures walk, crawl, or fly away with a full stomach, whereas the weaker creatures serve as nourishment for their adversaries.

Heavy clouds covering a full moon are hastily blown aside, allowing the moonlight to spill over the jungle greenery. Trees, bushes, and rocks become softly lit. With the illuminating moonlight, however, comes its counterpart—*the pitch-black shadows*—which are concealing hungry creatures waiting for sumptuous prey to stroll by.

Suddenly, a *saber-toothed tiger* bounds out of the shadows and catches *full sight of you.* Your gazes lock for a brief second. Adrenaline begins to gush through your system. Your instincts give you two viable options here. One, you can step up and battle-the-sucker (fight), or two, you can run-like-hell *(flight)!*

This is an example of the *fight-or-flight reaction.* The innate fight-or-flight mechanism is a survival reaction that is triggered by a threat. A fight-or-flight reaction is initiated by the primitive part of the brain, or paleo cortex. In prehistoric times, the fight-or-flight reaction was critically needed to ensure survival.

During the fight-or-flight reaction, there is an increase in arousal of both the body and the mind. Bodily arousal is accompanied by the release of hormones and increased muscle tension. Mind arousal manifests as anxiety that causes the adrenal glands to secrete adrenaline that, in turn, increases the heart rate, blood pressure, and causes other changes that over-stimulate the body and mind.

In today's world, the fight-or-flight reaction *is needed* when a would-be victim is cornered in an alley by a mugger. The victim protects him or herself by kicking the mugger during the assault *(fight)*. Similarly, the fight-or-flight reaction *is needed* when a woman is crossing a street and sees a car speeding toward her. The surge of adrenaline gives her the intense energy that she needs to get out of the oncoming car's path—quickly *(flight)*.

In contemporary life, however, the fight-or-flight reaction is only *occasionally* needed. Unfortunately, our primitive brains haven't evolved fast enough to know that *saber-toothed tigers are no longer a constant threat.* Thus, the primitive part of the brain frequently sets off fire alarms—when there are *no fires.* Often these alarms are simply modern life challenges that need more refined stress management tools than a *clunk-over-the-head* with a prehistoric club.

Varying Degrees of Stress

For most people, daily Stress Responses are *much subtler* than the acute fight-or-flight reactions that we just explored. When Stress Responses aren't acute, they may consist of worrisome thoughts and bodily tensions that are barely noticeable. The worrisome thoughts and bodily tensions may remain at bay while we're busy, then come into our awareness when we're no longer distracted. For example, our mind-body agitation may become noticeable when we're trying to relax or sleep.

Many of us experience varying degrees of Stress Responses to situations that aren't physically threatening, but feel *psychologically* threatening. For instance, let's say you get into an argument with a family member or your spouse. Neither of you are violent types, so clearly there is no threat to anyone's survival. However, due to the *emotional threat,* a Stress Response is triggered. That night, you find yourself unable to sleep as a result of the stress hormones your adrenal glands secreted earlier that day. In bed, you toss and turn as you replay the argument over and over in your mind. As you continue to feel agitated, you notice that your jaw is unusually tense.

This is a good example of how the mind and body fuel one another during a Stress Response. Worrying and having *scary thoughts* are the mind's way of *igniting* a Stress Response. Worrisome thoughts that include "always" and "never" are red flags for distorted thinking. All-or-nothing thinking is stressful because it tells us that whatever is wrong is black-and-white with absolutely no grays—*and no hope* of changing.

Another example of distorted thinking occurs when a thought that is overwhelmingly negative ends with a catastrophe. These extreme feelings are called *catastrophic thoughts.* Worrisome and catastrophic thoughts often begin with a, "*What if…?*"

So, while you are lying in bed unable to sleep after an argument, you may find yourself worrying:

"*What if* my spouse and I never resolve our differences?"

"We're always fighting, *what if* we end up getting divorced?"

"Then, *what if* I become ill and can't support myself?"

Whew! These catastrophic thoughts are *gold-foiled invitations* for adrenaline to pump.

An example of how scary thoughts can ignite a Stress Response relates to Carla who is a college student. She is an intelligent young woman who for two years has suffered with anxiety regarding taking tests. Her challenge is referred to as *Test Anxiety,* which is characterized by an apprehension of having one's performance judged or evaluated. Carla is stressed while studying for her upcoming biology test. Her anticipatory anxiety is creating *worrisome thoughts:*

"*What if* my mind goes blank while I'm taking the test?"

"*What if* I flunk the test?"

"*What if* I can't graduate due to lousy grades?"

As a result, if Carla doesn't use some stress-busting tools to counter her anticipatory anxiety, then there is a high probability that she will experience anxiety during the test taking. While studying for and taking tests, Carla has unintentionally turned her Stress Responses into a *vicious cycle.*

The following diagram illustrates the figure eight motion that results from a Stress Response perpetuating itself into a vicious cycle.

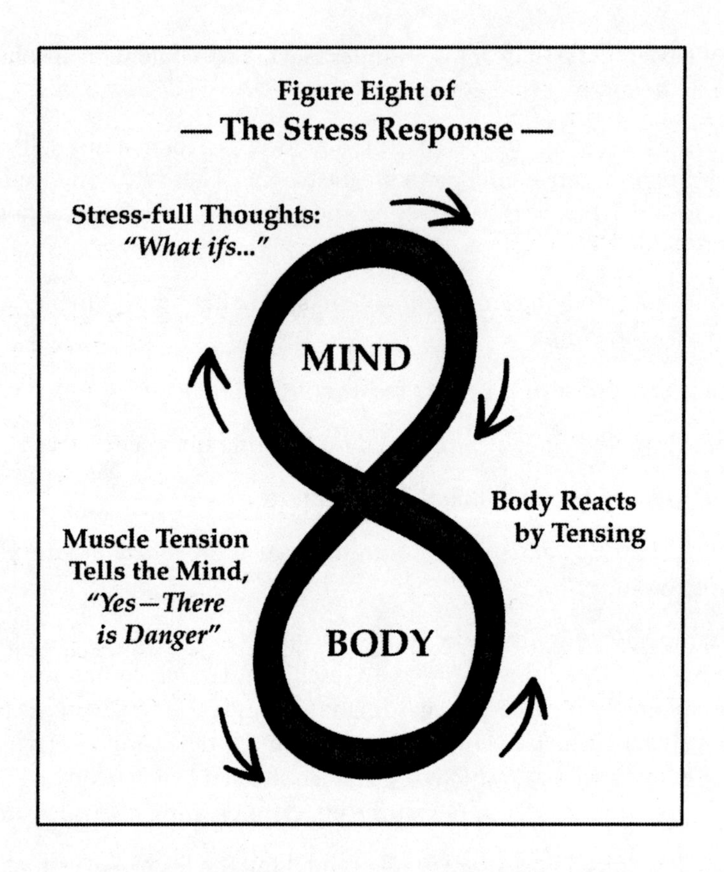

Now that we have clarified the role of the mind in creating a Stress Response, let's explore the role of the body. Bodily tension can *ignite* a Stress Response. Some of the *physiologic reflexes* that can happen during a fight-or-flight reaction are:

- Heart rate and blood pressure increase
- Blood vessels constrict to minimize bleeding in case the skin is punctured
- Bladder and rectum tense (and empty when extremely fearful)
- Muscles increase tension levels to prepare for fighting-or-fleeing
- Sweating increases
- Pupils dilate
- Jaw tenses
- Teeth clench
- Mouth dries

In his book, *Reversing Stress and Burnout,* Naras Bhat, M.D., F.A.C.P., describes how stress can be classified into three categories: Acute Stress, Chronic Stress, and Stress Addiction. Dr. Bhat says, "Acute Stress is a *fight-or-flight response* that includes the release of adrenaline. In its extreme, Acute Stress can lead to an 'anxiety attack' or full-blown panic."

For example, Bill is a Regional Sales Representative for a large software publisher. He spends at least two hours a day in the boardroom. On this particular day, the boardroom is hot and stuffy. The air conditioner is functioning poorly. Bill has been up since 2:00 a.m. preparing his sales report, which is due today. Bill's boss is short-tempered with everyone in the meeting.

The meeting drags on and Bill finds himself feeling increasingly agitated and tense *(fight).* One hour and forty-five minutes into the meeting, Bill notices that his palms are sweating and he is short of breath.

He has the momentary thought, "What if I get fired today?" He anxiously looks around the room. Then he realizes that his heart is racing.

"What if I'm having a heart attack?" he frantically asks himself.

With that, Bill feels an overwhelming urge to bolt from the conference room. Everything in him believes he is in *danger* and his racing mind is telling him, "*Red Alert—run!*" *(Flight).*

However, in this scenario, Bill *wasn't* going to get fired, and he *wasn't* having a heart attack. Bill was experiencing an Acute Stress Response, the fight-or-flight reaction, which then escalated into a full-blown panic attack.

And, unlike the prehistoric fight-or-flight scenario cited earlier, Bill's reaction wasn't suited to the circumstances that triggered it. There was no threat to Bill's physical safety or survival in that boardroom. No saber-toothed tigers attended the meeting that day. Therefore, he had no *rational* reason to fight-or-flee.

When an Acute Stress Response escalates into a panic attack, four (or more) of these symptoms occur abruptly and peak within ten minutes:

- Sweating
- Feeling short of breath or having smothering sensations
- Choking sensations
- Accelerated heart rate or palpitations

- Shaking or trembling
- Feeling unsteady, dizzy, lightheaded, or faint
- Abdominal distress or nausea
- Hot flashes or chills
- Tingling sensations or numbness
- Feeling detached or having a sense of unreality
- Chest pain or discomfort
- Fear of being out of control or going crazy
- Fear of dying

In Bill's example, did you notice that he had two scary or catastrophic, "What if…?" thoughts when his mind was overly aroused? They were:

"*What if* I get fired today?" (Fear of being out of control)

"*What if* I'm having a heart attack?" (Fear of dying)

Bill's scary thoughts fueled his Acute Stress Response, which then escalated into a panic attack. Likewise, when any of us ask ourselves scary questions that end in catastrophes, we are filling our imaginations with high drama. And let's face it—rarely, *if ever,* do our *fantasy fears* come true. So, then, 99.9% of the time, we are stewing our systems in stress chemicals for absolutely no reason.

In primitive times, when someone was experiencing a fight-or-flight reaction, they could utilize and discharge the stress hormones like adrenaline by fighting or running. By contrast, in modern times, if someone is experiencing a fight-or-flight reaction (or a panic attack) and they are confined to a boardroom or their car while in traffic, then the stress hormones don't have an effective way to be immediately utilized or discharged.

Bill's physical exhaustion, combined with his high muscle tension helped to fuel his panic attack at a body level. And according to numerous stress specialists, either a fight-or-flight reaction, or a full-blown panic attack *isn't dangerous.* When our mind-body fire alarms are wailing, it may *feel* as though we are in danger, *but in that moment we aren't*—we're simply geared up to fight-or-flee from *imaginary* saber-toothed tigers.

If stress becomes chronic, however, we may be living in a *continual cycle-of-alarm.* Chronic Stress *can* be dangerous to a person's health. Chronic Stress creates a cascade of hormones that includes insulin, cortisol, and testosterone. During Chronic Stress the body's physiology isn't given a chance to "return home" to the previous baseline of homeostasis. As a result, our exhausted and compromised immune systems can leave us vulnerable to stress-related disorders.

♦ ♦

Naras Bhat, M.D., F.A.C.P., says, "Stress addiction occurs when chronic stress and improper breathing create a vicious cycle. When people are stressed they often over-breathe, or hyperventilate. On the other extreme, some people hold their breaths when stressed. To correct this imbalance, many stress sufferers sigh or hyperventilate again, causing the stress addiction cycle to continue. These cycles of faulty breathing and unbalanced blood chemistry cause an influx of calcium, magnesium, and potassium. This can lead to many stress-related health problems such as insomnia, tense or painful muscles, chronic fatigue, rapid or irregular heartbeat, and coronary artery spasms. Other more psychological conditions that can be related to this cycle include excitability, panic, a restless mind, compulsive urges, phobias, excessive worry, fear, depression, and anger. And finally, the most insidious effect of faulty breathing and stress—is the immune system suppression—which greatly increases your risk for continual occurrences of infections, autoimmune disorders, heart disease, and cancer."

♦ ♦

The good news is that awareness of your stress levels and regular use of stress-busting tools will help you *interrupt* your unhealthy stress cycles and manage your stress better. Now do you see how the Stress Response is both a mind and a body issue? As you saw in the earlier Figure Eight Diagram, it's impossible to determine whether the mind starts the Stress Response, or if the body first instigates it. The age-old question might be appropriate here; *which came first, the chicken or the egg?*

For this reason, to counter Stress Responses, it is helpful to use tools that work at both mind and body levels. Fortunately, that is exactly where this chapter is headed! How about taking a nice, deep abdominal breath now in preparation for the upcoming *calming topic?*

The Relaxation Response

Like the Stress Response, the Relaxation Response is also a *body and mind issue.* At the body level, we move toward a Relaxation Response by *letting go* of muscle tension. By doing so, we are lengthening our muscle fibers by relaxing. Regular periods of relaxation allow our bodies to repair and recharge. As a result, we have a storehouse of energy to counter stress, and use for healing, when needed. *Letting go*—at both body and mind levels—decreases one's heart rate, blood pressure, and breathing rate.

At the mind level, we move toward a Relaxation Response by *letting go* of scary or worrisome thoughts. We catch our "What if…?" thoughts quickly and counter them with rational feedback to ourselves. Doing so switches us out of the *emotional* sides of our brains and into the *rational, logical* sides. As a result, we interrupt the worry cycle.

When Bill noticed he was having a Stress Response, he could have *coached himself* toward a Relaxation Response by first thinking, "I'm going to take some nice, deep, abdominal breaths now and imagine my body feeling as relaxed as cooked spaghetti." In addition to deep breathing, a *hearty helping of humor* is also an effective stress deflator.

Bill's survival instincts automatically searched for danger (a fire) when his *fight-or-flight alarms* were escalating. When he found nothing dangerous in his *environment,* Bill then turned his sentry toward his *body.*

"Aha!" his sentry exclaims, "My palms are sweating, I'm short of breath, and my heart is racing. I know there's danger! *What if* I'm having a heart attack?!"

To counter his "What if…?" thought, Bill could use a cognitive tool, and say to himself, "I was up late, I'm tired, and this room is hot. Just because my palms are moist, I'm breathing shallowly, and my heart is beating fast, *doesn't* mean I'm having a heart attack. I'm probably just pumping adrenaline and have *scared myself* into an anxiety attack. I'd better stop rattling myself with catastrophic thoughts. When I look around, I don't see a *single saber-toothed tiger* in this room."

Another worry-buster is to follow-up a "What if…?" with a light-hearted, "So what?" For example, if we catch ourselves *irrationally* thinking, "What if I get fired?" Our response might be, "So what? The sun will still come up tomorrow. I can ask for support from my loved ones and I'll network with other people in my profession. I won't starve and maybe I'll land a job that's more fulfilling. I know I'm safe right now, in this moment."

In short, Bill could counter his Stress Response by doing a simple, three-step process:

1. Breathe abdominally (body tool)
2. Check for bodily tension (body tool)
3. Counter negative or scary thoughts (mind tool)

The following Relaxation Response Diagram illustrates the figure eight motion that results when a person lets go of worrisome thoughts and body tension.

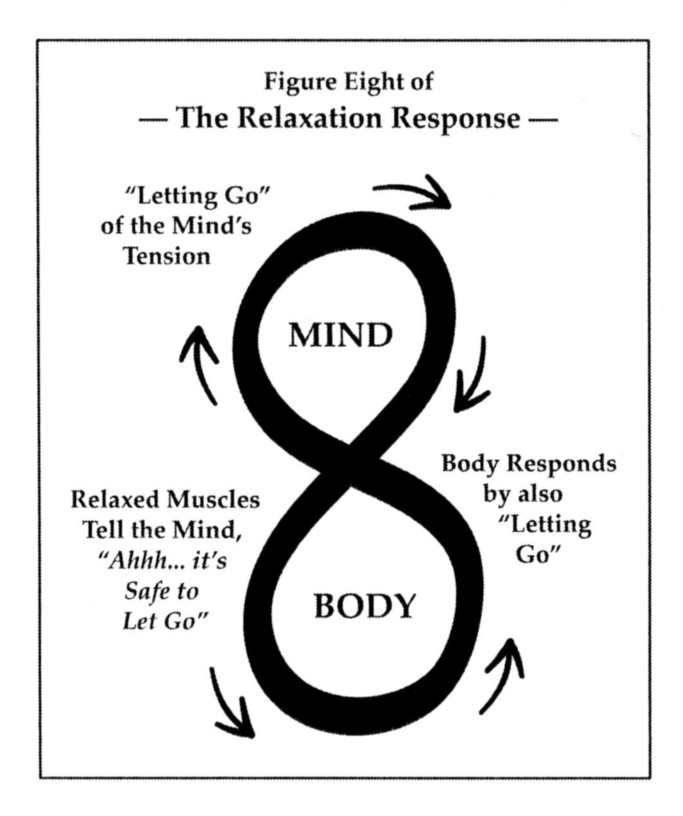

Finally, it is *tiger taming* time. If you're ready to learn how to identify the ways your mind and body may be fueling one another when you're stressed, then read on. This chapter, in addition to various other upcoming chapters, will guide you to tame those saber-toothed tiger responses. *Let's turn those "g-r-r-r…" reactions into "pur-r-r…" reactions!*

JOURNALING:

1. Meditate for a few minutes about how your *body fuels stress.* Here is a list of some common symptoms:

   - Tense shoulders
   - Tension around the eyes
   - Sweating
   - Shallow, upper-chest breathing
   - Heart rate speeds up
   - Jaw tension
   - Neck tension

   List some physical symptoms that you experience when you are stressed:

   -

   -

   -

   -

   -

2. Meditate for a few minutes about how your *mind fuels stress.* Think about a recent time you felt really stressed and see if you can identify some scary, or "What if…?" thoughts. Did you discover any *black-and-white thinking* containing "always" or "never?" Write your findings below and leave the space under each thought blank.

   a)

   b)

   c)

   d)

3. *Counter* each negative thought that you identified. Write your counter-response in the blank space that you left open below each scary thought.
4. To counter Stress Responses practice this simple, three-step process:
   1. Breathe abdominally (body tool)
   2. Check for bodily tension (body tool)
   3. Counter negative or scary thoughts (mind tool)
5. Complete this sentence through journaling:

   What's clear to me now is...

Inner Explorations and Inquiries...

Thoughts... Emotions... Memories... Sensations...

Inner Explorations and Inquiries...

Thoughts… Emotions… Memories… Sensations…

Inner Explorations and Inquiries...

Thoughts… Emotions… Memories… Sensations…

2

Coming Home

One of the gifts of having a meditation and journaling practice is the opportunity to *come home to ourselves* on a regular basis. We come home to ourselves when we shift our focus from outward distractions (such as television) and connect with what is going on inwardly. As a result, we learn to quiet our minds and bodies while lowering our stress levels and accessing our inner wisdom. Tapping into our "inside information" can assist us in having a mind-body connection while we are navigating the various twists and turns of our lives. Meditation and journaling are tools for self-care that help us *connect the conscious with the unconscious.*

Another tool to increase our conscious awareness is *guided imagery.* Guided imagery is a form of meditation that uses creative visualization to discover our inner healing resources. In addition to conventional medical treatment, many practitioners are using guided imagery with their patients to explore physical, emotional, and behavioral issues. These include heart disease, cancer, weight loss, stress and pain management, smoking cessation, addiction recovery, and healing childhood traumas.

Guided imagery is *not* a substitute for traditional medical care, but it can be a complementary treatment. Obtain a diagnosis and treatment plan from your doctor before seeking complementary methods. In addition, if you feel unsure about your doctor's diagnosis, then seek a second and even a third opinion. Keep in mind, you may be putting yourself in danger if you are using *only* self-healing techniques.

Although guided imagery's usage is common today; it is not a new tool. An Italian psychiatrist, Roberto Assagioli (1888-1975), used imagery techniques and meditation extensively. He was the founder of *Psychosynthesis,* a spiritual psychology used to synthesize the various parts of a person's personality and *create harmony* within the psyche.

Many scientific studies in recent years validate the mind-body connection. O. Carl Simonton, a radiation oncologist, and his wife, Stephanie Matthews-Simonton, a psychologist, increased the use of meditation and imagery in the medical world in the late 1960s. Their reports showed that cancer patients who used meditation and guided imagery to increase their immune system responses lived longer than those who did not.

In the next section, you will see specific examples of the powerful connection between the mind and the body. In addition, you will have an opportunity to work with a guided imagery tool that can assist you in turning Stress Responses into Relaxation Responses.

Creating Conditioned Relaxation Responses

Now it is time to explore two types of responses. First we will focus on *unconditioned responses* and then turn our attentions to *conditioned responses.* Clearly, we all have built-in responses to various stimuli. For example, if functioning properly, our eyes respond to light in a consistent way. When a ray of light hits our eyes, our pupils respond by contracting or shrinking. This response is built-in, unconditioned, and automatic. The flow of saliva triggered by food in the mouth is another example of an unconditioned, or automatic, response.

Likewise, if you have had a physical recently you might remember the doctor tapping you below the kneecap. Your leg responded to the tap by swinging out. This is another form of an unconditioned response. Here are the examples simplified:

—Unconditioned Responses—	
Stimulus:	**Response:**
Light shined into eye	Pupil contracts
Food placed into mouth	Saliva flows
Doctor taps below kneecap	Leg swings out

In 1904, the Russian scientist, Ivan Pavlov (1849-1936) won the Nobel Prize in Physiology. Pavlov studied the conditioning of saliva secretion of dogs. Pavlov presented food to hungry dogs and then measured and recorded the flow of saliva. When he repeatedly rang a bell each time that he presented food to the hungry dogs, they salivated. After a while, Pavlov no longer showed the dogs any food and only rang a bell. At the sound of the bell, the dogs' mouths watered—even without *any* food present.

Pavlov called this newly learned response a *conditioned response.* The dogs learned to connect an unconditioned *stimulus* to a *response.* Thanks to Pavlov's work, scientists have determined that much of the behavior of humans and lower animals is conditioned. For example, have you ever heard a song play on the radio that changed your mood? Perhaps a love song reminded you of being young and infatuated. Simply hearing the song may have changed your mood from bored to romantic and nostalgic.

Commercial advertising attempts to create *conditioned responses* in their audience. The goal of the advertiser is to trigger a viewer's automatic response to a stimulus so that the viewer will buy the product. They want an emotion associated with their product. Feeling attractive, happy, energetic, popular, and loving are some common emotional responses that advertisers attempt to *condition the viewers to associate with their products.*

Have you noticed how many thin actors there are in TV commercials who are eating fattening foods like candy bars, ice cream, and pizza? Yep, that skinny, acne-free actor is ecstatically savoring the food he is eating. The advertiser shows the alluring close-ups of the caramel or the pizza cheese stringing sensuously from the actor's smiling lips. It comes as no surprise that the relationship between an over-consumption of sugary foods to obesity or diabetes is nowhere to be seen in these seductive commercials.

The good news is, there are ways to use conditioned responses to increase health and well-being. For example, empowering tools such as meditation, guided imagery, and journaling are excellent methods to counter Stress Responses and move toward Relaxation Responses. To create a Relaxation Response, meditation and guided imagery often include *anchors* (conditioned responses) to help people return to their relaxed states. Likewise, choosing a consistent place to meditate and practice guided imagery can assist in the creation of an anchor. As a result, sitting down on the meditation chair or cushion becomes a triggering stimulus that can lead to a relaxed state.

I do guided imagery to assist clients in relaxing deeply. After the person is relaxed, I suggest that he or she *anchor* the calm state through a hand gesture. A simple movement like touching a thumb to an index finger is chosen. Later my client can easily do the simple hand gesture while sitting in traffic or under the table at a business board meeting. Combining the *hand gesture* with *belly breathing,* while thinking the word *calm,* can serve as stimuli to counter a Stress Response and invite in a Relaxation Response. In this way, Pavlov's discoveries can serve to *increase* a person's ability to manage him or herself at both mind and body levels.

Think about the positive possibilities that could result for people who learn to counter their Stress Responses creatively. For instance, people who have fears of public speaking could literally alter the course of their lives by learning to manage their mind-body reactions. Teaching or inspirational speaking are simply two choices they might pursue as a result of overcoming their fears.

—Conditioned Responses—	
Stimulus:	**Response:**
Bell is rung	Pavlov's dog salivates
Love song on radio	Nostalgic, romantic feeling
Candy bar or pizza on TV	Hunger/craving for the product
Meditation or guided imagery	Relaxation Response by letting go of mind & muscle tension
Relaxation anchor	Relaxation Response by letting go of mind & muscle tension
Stress	Relaxation anchor to assist in creating a Relaxation Response

A guided imagery exercise is included in this chapter to assist you in turning *Stress Responses into Relaxation Responses.* You can follow the script that will teach you to relax deeply. Then you will be invited to take a journey to a Sacred Place. When you are relaxed in your Sacred Place, you will have an opportunity to *anchor* this relaxed and calm state. By regularly using your anchor, you can put the scientific findings of Pavlov and his "drooling dogs" to work for you.

If you would like to discover your Sacred Place, then read the following *guided imagery script.* Know that, even if you don't find a Sacred Place within the first few times you practice the exercise, you're not doing anything wrong.

When you are ready to do this exercise, read the guided imagery script *slowly and calmly* into a cassette recorder (or record it onto a CD if you have this computer capability). If you don't have a recorder, then consider asking a friend if he or she has one you can use.

You will see three *pause prompts* throughout the guided imagery script. Here are time suggestions for each:

1. "…": Pause briefly for two or three seconds
2. *(Pause):* Pause approximately five to ten seconds
3. *(Pause, turn off tape if you need extra time)*: Take the time that you need

Play back the recording for yourself when you have approximately twenty uninterrupted minutes. *Never* listen to your recording while you are driving a motor vehicle, operating equipment, or doing anything that requires your concentration and attention. Know that, if an emergency occurs while you are using your tape, that you can quickly and easily bring yourself to full alertness (and out of the focused, relaxed state) by counting yourself back from three to one.

Guided Imagery Script:

Coming Home to Your Inner Sanctuary

1. Sit comfortably in a chair…Center yourself by sitting in an upright position…You may want to uncross your arms and legs so that you can easily relax into the guided imagery experience.

2. Feel the weight of your feet connecting to the floor…Let your thighs relax…Allow your weight to sink into the chair you're sitting on…Give yourself permission to be held fully and completely by the chair…Feel your spine supported by the chair…Know that Mother Earth is also holding your chair fully and completely.

3. Think about a color that feels relaxing and peaceful to you…Imagine this color as a beautiful border of light surrounding the room you're sitting in.

4. Follow your breath as it enters through your nostrils and moves into your lungs...After observing your breathing for a few minutes, see if you can deepen it into your belly.

(Pause, turn off tape if you need extra time)

5. Now get a sense of any burdens, tensions, or worries that you're carrying on your shoulders or back...If you feel some, then in your mind's eye, give your burdens a form...Visualize (or sense) what your burdens look or feel like...For example, sacks of coal or bricks may represent your burdens...Feel their weight...then, gently pull your shoulders up toward your ears and hold for a count of three...

Next, imagine your worries and burdens sliding off into Mother Earth—where they can serve as fuel...Let gravity pull all the burdens down off your shoulders and say aloud or to yourself, "Ah-h-h..." as you exhale and lower your shoulders...Imagine the sound of the burdens as they drop to the earth and dissipate...Repeat a few times...Invite in the freedom and relief that come from releasing your burdens...Envision a beautifully colored light filling the space that you've created...where the burdens once were.

6. Shift your attention now and imagine yourself walking along a path...The path can be in a forest setting, along a beach, or any place that feels comfortable to you...Since you're the creator of this imagery, know that you can choose any kind of path you want...See or sense the surface that you're walking on...Feel the textures under your toes...As you imagine yourself taking each step, allow yourself to relax deeper and deeper.

(Pause)

7. See or sense whatever is surrounding you on your path...Notice if there are any sounds in your environment...If so, what are they?

(Pause)

What scents or smells do you notice in the air?

8. As you walk along your path, know that you can invite in any *positive resources* that you choose to bring with you on this journey...Invite in whatever or whomever you need, as long as they feel comforting and supportive of you...You can invite in a loved one, a spiritual figure, and/or, any animal that feels compassionate and safe...In addition, if you'd like a walking stick or a shawl, invite in whatever *feels good to you.*

(Pause, turn off tape if you need extra time)

9. Continue moving along your path...You might notice that there are some stairs up ahead that are carved out of your path...If it feels right, then give yourself permission to walk down the stairs...Feel each foot stepping down...down...down...into deeper...and deeper relaxation...Let yourself know that when you reach the bottom of the stairs you will be deeply relaxed.

(Pause)

10. As you move along the level path again...you may see in the distance that there is a curve in the road...Around the bend of the curve is *your Sacred Place*...Know that, you are the *architect* of your Sacred Place, therefore, you can choose to create *any* environment you want...Your Sacred Place can be a cottage, a castle, a cave, an open natural environment—like a beach, a forest, a garden, a tree house—or anyplace else that feels comfortable to you.

11. As you walk around the bend, allow your Sacred Place to appear...Consider letting this special place *call you home*...As you continue to move closer, let more details of your Sacred Place become clearer...When you've arrived at the entrance, pause and imagine yourself taking a moment of silence.

(Pause)

When you are ready, feel your feet taking you into your Sacred Place...Let the energy of this place *welcome you home.*

12. If it feels right, bring in any of the resources that you invited along with you earlier...Look around and see or sense what is there.

(Pause)

Notice if there are any sounds in your Sacred Place...If so, what are they? What scents are in your environment?

13. Since you're the designer of your Sacred Place, what would you like to invite in so that you feel even *more relaxed...comfortable...and at home?* Is there a place to sit or lie? If not, create a chair or a bed for yourself...Don't skimp, let your imagination run positively wild...If a throne, a sparkling recliner, a swing, a hammock, or a feather bed appeals to you, then invite it in....and, if simplicity feels better, then honor that choice.

(Pause)

Now, sit or lie in your chair, bed, hammock, or whatever you've created… this is your *Relaxing Spot.*

14. What else would you like to invite into your Sacred Place? Some flowers perhaps? A bookshelf full of interesting books? Take some time to follow the *guidance of your heart,* and have fun decorating your Sacred Place.

(Pause, turn off tape if you need extra time)

Now, from your Relaxing Spot, see if there is anything else that will calm and comfort you *even further…*Bring in whatever you like…Bathe in the relaxation you've created…You might want to imagine that the relaxation is *showering* over…around…and through you…Invite in this nourishing energy…to wherever you choose.

15. Now *anchor this calm and relaxed state* by gently touching two of your fingers together…a thumb and an index finger are fine, or some other simple gesture that you choose…This hand gesture will serve as your *connector* to your Sacred Place…your anchor…so, when you touch your fingers together…or do whatever gesture you've chosen, you will *easily connect with a calm and relaxed state.*

Now relax your hand/s again.

16. Look around your sacred environment and see, or sense, if there is a message there for you. For example, the message may appear inside *a boxed gift* that you open…or appear on a piece of paper that's tucked inside *a bottle…*or you may spontaneously open *a book* to a specific page and find a message…You may *see, sense,* or *hear a message…*Let your imagination be free to receive in whatever form is right for you…Take a minute or two now to see if there is a message for you, somewhere in your Sacred Place.

(Pause, turn off tape if you need extra time)

And, if no message revealed itself, be willing to receive the message in the next few days or weeks ahead…not everyone experiences a message in the moment…so don't pressure or judge yourself if no message came through.

17. It's time to journey back now, so, in preparation…you might want to take a moment to offer *gratitude to your Sacred Place…*and, know that, you're bringing your Sacred Place back with you…Since you created and claimed it—*your Sacred Place belongs to you.*

18. To bring your Sacred Place back with you, imagine that it is becoming *transparent...*See or sense yourself walking outside of your Sacred Place and standing at its entrance...Imagine that it is now shrinking down to a size that will fit inside your chest, your heart, or into your pocket...See or sense yourself transforming it into an *Inner Sanctuary...*Breathe deeply into your *precious internalized sanctuary.*

(Pause)

19. Know that you can access your Inner Sanctuary, *easily,* whenever you need a moment of calming relaxation...Simply touch the two fingers together that you anchored earlier...In the days, weeks, and months ahead, give yourself permission to *easily connect* with your Inner Sanctuary.

20. Return to your path now and see or sense yourself walking along it. As you move along the path, bring all the resources that you invited in earlier, back with you...When you arrive at the stairs that are cut into the path, begin stepping up...With each step you take, you will feel an increase in *alertness and energy...*Move up one step at a time, with each step you will feel increased energy...and feel more...and even more...*refreshed and renewed.*

(Pause)

21. At the top of the stairs, continue along your level path again. Know that, you will easily remember *everything* from your journey and that you can continue to glean insights from it. You will be counted back now from ten to one. At *one*, or whenever you are ready...you can open your eyes and return to your environment feeling refreshed and renewed...*Ten...nine...*more energy, *eight...seven...*more alertness, *six...five...*halfway back, *four...three...*almost back, *two...*and *one.*

22. Welcome yourself back now by taking a few nice, deep abdominal breaths.

Take plenty of time to reorient. Since you were in a deeply relaxed state, allow yourself time to feel grounded before driving or performing any activities that require high skill and alertness.

When you're ready, complete the following exercises:

JOURNALING:

1. Write about your experience of journeying to your Sacred Place. What resources did you invite along with you? Describe what you saw or sensed in your Sacred Place.

If resistance came up, and you were unable to go to a Sacred Place, then write about this experience. Try to be compassionate with yourself, rather than judgmental. Know that resistance can be an important teacher that offers useful information.

2. If a message came through while you were in your Sacred Place, then write about it.

3. Complete this sentence through journaling:

What's clear to me now is…

Thoughts... Emotions... Memories... Sensations...

Inner Explorations and Inquiries...

Thoughts... Emotions... Memories... Sensations...

Inner Explorations and Inquiries...

Thoughts... Emotions... Memories... Sensations...

3

Inner Wisdom

Have you ever *sensed something* that surprisingly turned out to be true? Maybe you had a feeling that someone was dangerous and later found out that you were right. Instinctual, or intuitive, messages can surface from deep within as a gut response, an inner knowing, or a hunch. In addition to giving you a message about someone or something external, your intuition can also be useful in getting information related to your personal health. If you want to develop your intuition consciously, meditation and guided imagery can be excellent ways to move toward this goal.

We all have built-in instincts that give us important information about our health and well-being, that is, *if we are listening.* Unfortunately, when we are continuously focused outside ourselves we may miss hearing that still, small voice that is seeking our attention. Occasionally, the volume of the instinctual message is turned up—so that we hear it *loud and clear.*

Author Martin L. Rossman, M.D., is a pioneer in the field of mind-body imagery. He teaches patients and health care professionals how to use imagery for healing. In *Guided Imagery for Self-Healing,* he says, "Having a talk with an imaginary wise figure—an Inner Advisor—may sound strange, yet doing it is one of the most powerful techniques I know for helping you understand the relationships between your thoughts, feelings, actions, and health."

♦ ♦

One of my standard practices for the last five years has been connecting to my Inner Consultant or Advisor through meditation. When I honor that my Inner Consultant has important input regarding my health and well-being, I own my personal power. Does this mean I can't ask for feedback from others, too? Absolutely not. Seeking assistance for a particular challenge from "an expert" or medical specialist is a given. In fact, my Inner Consultant has pointed me in that direction numerous times. When I'm facing a challenge, I gather *outer resources* that I use in addition to my *inner resources.*

Accessing my Inner Consultant has gotten easier over time. When the need arises, I sit and begin to meditate. For the first few minutes I observe my breathing and deepen it into my abdomen. After becoming relaxed and centered, I imagine a mountain in front of me. I visualize myself easily climbing to the top where my Inner Consultant is waiting. We sit together and I ask for feedback on whatever issue is stirring in my life. Then I quietly wait to see if an answer comes. As odd as this may sound, I feel calm while in the presence of my Inner Consultant.

Sometimes the feedback I receive comes through loud and clear. However, at other times, haziness prevents me from getting an answer. When the fog shows up, I still feel good in the presence of my Inner Consultant and simply trust that the answers and clarity will come in their own time. The fog usually clears within a day or two and clarity comes to me.

I use the mountaintop imagery to connect with my Inner Consultant because it offers a higher perspective. In my mind's eye, I can look down and see a bigger picture. The higher vision helps me to rise above the challenge and get beyond the minutiae.

♦ ♦

Keep in mind, the feedback that you receive from your Inner Consultant needs to be considered mindfully. Trust develops over time. Dr. Rossman cautions, "You may find it reassuring to know that while you do want to know what your advisor has to say, you don't have to do anything it recommends…. You will evaluate the risks and benefits of following its advice and make your own decision…. Don't abandon your responsibility to your Inner Advisor, but consider what it has to tell you."

The Inner Consultant can be an internal ally who bridges the connection between the *conscious and unconscious minds.* When I use guided imagery to assist my clients in connecting with their Inner Consultants, the forms that appear are often dramatically different from one another. Some of the forms that appear include a Wise Woman or Man, a beloved spiritual figure, an animal, a plant, a nurturing relative or teacher from the person's past. Like symbols in dreams, the form that someone's inner guidance takes is *profoundly personal.*

One of my clients, whom we'll call Sandra, initially had a difficult time connecting with her Inner Consultant. While in a relaxed meditative state, she kept waiting for it to appear in front of her. After repeated attempts, her Inner Consultant finally came through as a voice from a beautifully painted shield that covered her heart and belly. In one of our sessions, she received valuable feedback from her shield telling her how to be *visible and empowered* in the world. Sandra is a shy person and this protective shield helped her to feel more confident at work—especially when she needed to make presentations to large groups. Sandra's Inner Consultant continues to be a rich resource in her life. She is grateful for the ability to access this powerful internal ally.

An essential guideline for *accepting* an Inner Consultant is seeing or sensing love and safety while in its presence. If through the upcoming guided imagery script, you connect with an Inner Consultant, then you will have an opportunity to *interview it.* If the "candidate" that comes forth has eyes, then look into them. In the eyes of a *truly loving* Inner Consultant, you will see or sense *compassion and care.* If these qualities aren't present, then explore it like you would a character in a dream—with respect and curiosity. Even if it's *not* your Inner Consultant, it may have some useful information for you.

Now think about a simple, light-hearted question that you can ask your Inner Consultant during the guided imagery. Choose a question that isn't highly charged. For example, Janice is a thirty-year old single woman who would love to find someone for a long-term relationship. Her first question to her Inner Consultant was, "How can I meet more men who share some of my interests?" Janice's Inner Consultant suggested that she talk with her minister about inviting other members of the church to create a Singles Hiking Group. She could organize the group and ask her minister to list its activities in the church's monthly newsletter. Janice was pleased with the feedback she received in response to her question and decided to follow up with her minister. As you can see, Janice's first simple question wasn't emotionally charged. Wisely, she did not ask her Inner Consultant whether she would be unmarried and alone for the rest of her life—since this would have been a highly charged question.

So if you are ready to invite your Inner Consultant into your awareness, read the following guided imagery script. Know that, even if you don't make a connection the first few times you practice the exercise—you're not doing anything wrong.

When you are ready to do this exercise, read the guided imagery script *slowly and calmly* into a cassette recorder (or record it onto a CD if you have this computer capability). If you don't have a recorder, then consider asking a friend if he or she has one you can use.

You will see three *pause prompts* throughout the guided imagery script. Here are time suggestions for each:

1. "...": Pause briefly for two or three seconds
2. *(Pause):* Pause approximately five to ten seconds
3. *(Pause, turn off tape if you need extra time)*: Take the time that you need

Play back the recording for yourself when you have approximately twenty uninterrupted minutes. *Never* listen to your recording while you are driving a motor vehicle, operating equipment, or doing anything that requires your concentration and attention. Know that, if an emergency occurs while you are using your tape, that you can quickly and easily bring yourself to full alertness (and out of the focused, relaxed state) by counting yourself back from three to one.

Guided Imagery Script:

Connecting with Your Inner Consultant

1. Sit comfortably in a chair...Center yourself by sitting in an upright position...You may want to uncross your arms and legs so that you can easily relax into the guided imagery experience.

2. Feel the weight of your feet connecting to the floor...Let your thighs relax...Allow your weight to sink into the chair you're sitting on...Give yourself permission to be held fully and completely by the chair...Feel your spine supported by the chair.

3. Think about a *color* that feels relaxing and peaceful to you...Imagine this relaxing color entering through your nostrils and moving down into your lungs as you inhale...and exhale...On the next breath, let the relaxation move into your belly...See or sense the relaxation expanding from your belly...and filling all your extremities...down your legs...all the way into the tips of your toes.

(Pause)

4. Let the relaxation now move upward and expand into your arms...all the way into your fingertips...Notice if your hands have any tension...If they do...consider giving your hands permission to relax and let go...Let your hands know that it is safe to hold life lightly and gently.

(Pause)

5. As you've done before...get a sense of any burdens, tensions, or worries that you're carrying on your shoulders or back...If you feel some, then in your mind's eye, give your burdens a form...Visualize (or sense) what your burdens look or feel like...For example, sacks of coal or bricks may represent your burdens...Feel their weight...then, gently pull your shoulders up toward your ears and hold for a count of three.

Next, imagine your worries and burdens sliding off into Mother Earth—where they can serve as fuel...Let gravity pull all the burdens down off your shoulders and say aloud or to yourself, "Ah-h-h..." as you exhale and lower your shoulders...Imagine the sound of the burdens as they drop to the earth and dissipate...Repeat a few times...Invite in the freedom and relief that come from releasing your burdens...Envision a beautifully colored light filling the space that you've created...where the burdens once were.

6. Shift your attention now and imagine yourself walking along a path that leads to your *Sacred Place*...See or sense the surface that you are walking on...Feel the textures under your toes...As you imagine taking each step, allow yourself to relax deeper and deeper.

(Pause)

What scents or smells do you notice in the air?

7. As you move along your path, know that you can invite in any *positive resources* that you choose to bring with you on this journey...They can be the same as you chose for the first guided imagery or include different supportive resources...For example, you can invite in a loved one, a spiritual figure, and/or, any animal that feels compassionate and safe...Again, invite in whatever or whomever you need, as long as they feel comforting and supportive to you.

8. Continue moving along your path...and when you get to a set of stairs that are carved out of your path...if it feels right, then walk down the stairs...Feel each foot stepping down...down...down...into deeper...and

deeper relaxation…Let yourself know that when you reach the bottom of the stairs you will be deeply relaxed.

(Pause)

9. As you move along the level path again, you will see a curve in the road…Around the bend of the curve is *your Sacred Place…*When you get to the entrance, take a moment of silence…then enter.

10. Get connected to your Sacred Place…Look around and see or sense the peacefulness of this environment…When you're ready…sit or lie in your Relaxing Spot.

11. If you feel deeply relaxed right now…*anchor the relaxation* by doing the hand configuration that you chose earlier…Think *c-a-l-m* as you gently bathe in the relaxation.

(Pause)

Now relax your hand/s again.

12. From this calm state…when you're ready…invite your *Inner Consultant* to come to you in your Sacred Place…Be open to having your Inner Consultant appear before you in whatever shape spontaneously forms…Know that it may come in a variety of forms…perhaps a Wise Woman or Man, a person, animal, or symbol representing your Higher Self, a beloved spiritual figure, a plant, a nurturing relative or teacher from your past.

The only requirement for your Inner Consultant is that it be compassionate, caring, and supportive of you…Know that, it first may appear hazy and pale…Relax and let the image clarify itself to you…Take your time now as you patiently wait to see if your Inner Consultant is ready to join you.

(Pause, turn off tape if you need extra time)

13. If your Inner Consultant has joined you…then invite it to sit comfortably with you in your Sacred Place…You might ask if it has a name.

(Pause)

If your Inner Consultant has eyes…look deeply into them and see if *kindness and compassion* reside there…If your Inner Consultant doesn't have eyes…simply *sense* if it is kind and compassionate toward you.

14. If you sense that the Inner Consultant is kind and compassionate...then consider asking it your simple question...As suggested earlier, since you're getting acquainted with your Inner Consultant, choose a question that is light-hearted...Wait quietly and patiently now for an answer.

(Pause, turn off tape if you need extra time)

15. If a response comes through...then think about the advice...Imagine taking the advice...Do any possible negative consequences come into your mind?

(Pause)

If so, then share these thoughts with your Inner Consultant...Brainstorm for as long as you need.

(Pause, turn off tape if you need extra time)

16. When you're ready...thank your Inner Consultant for its input...You might want to offer it a *moment of gratitude*...Say goodbye in whatever way feels good...a touch of hands, a hug, or a smile...however you'd like to close this meeting...And, know that, you're bringing your Inner Consultant back with you...to connect with whenever you choose.

17. Get back on your path now and see or sense yourself walking...as you move along the path, bring all the resources that you invited in earlier...back with you...including your Inner Consultant...When you get to the stairs that are cut into the path, begin stepping up...With each step up that you take, you will feel an increase in *alertness and energy*...move up...one step at a time...With each step you'll feel increased energy...and feel more...and even more...*refreshed and renewed.*

(Pause)

18. At the top of the stairs, continue along your level path again. Know that, you will easily remember *everything* from your journey and that you can continue to glean insights from it. You will be counted back now from ten to one. At *one*, or whenever you are ready...you can open your eyes and return to your environment feeling refreshed and renewed...*Ten*...*nine*...more energy, *eight*...*seven*...more alertness, *six*...*five*...halfway back, *four*...*three*...almost back, *two*...and *one*.

19. Welcome yourself back now by taking a few nice, deep abdominal breaths.

Take plenty of time to reorient. Since you were in a deeply relaxed state, allow yourself time to feel grounded before driving or performing any activities that require high skill and alertness.

Assessing Your Inner Consultant and Its Advice

How was your experience? If an Inner Consultant came to you, did you see or sense that it was compassionate, loving, and caring toward you? As you assess the experience of meeting your Inner Consultant, keep in mind that we all have a variety of internal selves that make up our personalities. That's why, for example, if you have a strong Pusher/Doer (goal-oriented) self, then its advice may prompt you to achieve more, more, *and more.* Although it's great to have inner conversations with an inner Pusher/Doer, it's not a good candidate to serve as a wise Inner Consultant because its perspective isn't broad or high enough.

For this reason, it is advisable to check out carefully who or what showed up to give you feedback. Gently become acquainted with it and ask simple questions for a while. As mentioned earlier, know that you don't have to follow any advice you receive from your Inner Consultant if it doesn't feel right or if the impact on your life would be dramatic. Let your trust develop over time. You will also want to consider what impact following the advice from your Inner Consultant may have on others in your life. Consult with those who could be affected by your choice of action. Mindfulness is the key here.

Congratulations on taking the first step toward developing your *internal power partner,* the Inner Consultant. Turning up the volume on the still, small voice within can be a rich asset to receive feedback from regarding various aspects of your life. Consider your work here to be an investment in reclaiming a valuable personal resource—*a direct line to your inner wisdom.*

When you're ready, complete the following exercises:

JOURNALING:

1a. Write about your experience of inviting in your Inner Consultant. (If you didn't experience an Inner Consultant, then skip to 1b). Describe what you saw or sensed as the process unfolded. Was your Inner Consultant kind and compassionate toward you? What question did you ask it? Did you get an answer? Are there any risks or possible negative consequences that you need to weigh before considering whether to take the advice?

1b. If an Inner Consultant didn't come to you, then write about this experience. Try to be compassionate with yourself, rather than judgmental. Know that whatever you experienced is important information. If an energy or character came through that wasn't kind or compassionate, write about it.

Could this be a part of yourself that needs some attention or healing? Would it benefit you to get support from a qualified therapist?

Also, if you aren't successful in accessing an Inner Consultant after a few attempts, then, for an in-depth discussion, consider reading Dr. Martin Rossman's book, *Guided Imagery for Self-Healing*. If an Inner Critic showed up in your journey, Hal and Sidra Stone's book, *Embracing Your Inner Critic* might be a good resource to check out as well.

2. Complete this sentence through journaling:

What's clear to me now is…

Inner Explorations and Inquiries…

Thoughts... Emotions... Memories... Sensations...

Inner Explorations and Inquiries...

Thoughts… Emotions… Memories… Sensations…

Inner Explorations and Inquiries...

Thoughts... Emotions... Memories... Sensations...

4

What's Buggin' Me?

It seems as though this question *should* be easy to answer. After all, most of us are intelligent adults who can make decisions, reason, and problem solve. But the truth is, cognitive intelligence differs greatly from emotional intelligence.

An expanded theory of intelligence began brewing when Harvard Professor, Howard Gardner, challenged the widely accepted belief that intelligence is based only on one's "I.Q." (Intelligence Quotient) or thinking abilities. In 1983, his theory of intelligence was published as *Frames of Mind: The Theory of Multiple Intelligences.* Gardner's innovative model included these nine forms of intelligence: bodily/kinesthetic, musical/rhythmic, logical/mathematical, verbal/linguistic, visual/spatial, naturalist, existentialist, interpersonal emotions ("socially smart"), and intrapersonal emotions ("self smart").

In 1995, best-selling author, Daniel Goleman's, *Emotional Intelligence: Why it can matter more than I.Q.*, broadened this theory of intelligence even further. Goleman added "E.Q." (Emotional Quotient) to I.Q. His model includes impulse control, self-awareness, empathy, social skills, zeal, self-motivation, and persistence. He illustrates how people of high intelligence sometimes flounder at work, whereas others with a modest I.Q., but high E.Q., are surprisingly successful.

So in addition to conventional I.Q.—for optimal health and success—today we need high E.Q. "Fluency regarding emotions?" you may protest. Yes, the truth is, if we want balanced physical and mental health, then emotional intelligence is important. *Whew, I bet you didn't see this one coming!* While most of us studied reading, writing, and arithmetic when we were in school, the importance of emotional intelligence as a "life skill" was circulating somewhere in the ether.

Fortunately, some kids today *are* learning life skills that include *self-science.* Emotional intelligence classes have moved into the educational system and currently thousands of schools worldwide are teaching emotional literacy in their curriculums. That's the good news! But, those of us who didn't learn these important life skills in school are left seeking our own means of education. That's where this journal comes in; its numerous chapters offer tools that increase emotional intelligence.

As mentioned earlier, meditation is a great way to access our inner landscapes and thus increase our E.Q. When we use a repetitive sound or mantra, we are giving ourselves permission to disengage from the busy mind. We move away from simply feeling like a *human doing* into experiencing ourselves as a *human being.* Included in the human being experience is a range of emotions. *All* of the emotions—the powerful ones and the vulnerable ones. "Oy vey," you may reply, "not those *whiney ones?*"

If you were ever a Saturday Night Live fan in its earlier days, you'll probably remember Bill Murray in his turquoise-colored leisure suit singing, "Feelings." He definitely played up the emotionality of vulnerable feelings as the lounge-lizard character. This was one hilarious sketch! I'm giggling just remembering the expression on his face while he sang. Murray scrunched his eyebrows together and looked as though he might be trying to pass a kidney stone! So, if I assure you that belting out the chorus of "Feelings" won't be required here—will you continue reading?

Great, you're still with me. In our healthy quest for increased self-awareness, let's explore some emotions now. Seven basic emotions are:

• Love	• Fear
• Joy	• Anger
	• Worry
	• Guilt
	• Sadness

You may notice the list under fear is much longer than the list under love. In this chapter we will be focusing on the tougher feelings more than the warm fuzzies. Other chapters, however, will assist you in exploring feelings of joy and love, as well as, how to connect deeply with others.

Love and fear are the primary emotions for the feelings you see listed below them. Love moves us toward people, places, or things; it is an expanding emotion. Therefore, love comes from our desire to connect. On the other hand, fear moves us away from people, places, or things; it is a contracting emotion. Fear comes from our instinctive desire to protect and survive.

Joy is an emotion related to love. When we feel joy, love is involved. Many people feel joyful during activities or hobbies they love. For example, Laura feels joy when she plays her violin. She has loved classical music since she was a little girl. So there is clearly a *love component* related to her joy.

By contrast, anger, worry, guilt, and sadness are basic emotions related to fear. They often have a *fear component* underlying them. For example, if you've ever had a car abruptly cut you off on the freeway, you may have felt an urge to wave your fist out the window. You probably had an increased heart rate and felt angry that the other driver nearly got you into an accident! If you stay angry about this incident, you may ignore the fact that you first felt fear—which was quickly followed by anger. Since fear came first, it was the primary emotion, whereas, anger was the secondary emotion.

To illustrate this, let's use the example of a Barrel Cactus. The prickly parts that you see above ground represent anger. Below ground is where the roots are holding the vulnerable emotions like worry, guilt, sadness, and fear. If you stay focused on what you're aware of above ground, the prickly parts or the anger, you may find yourself becoming painfully stuck! And in case you haven't heard—chronic anger is an *extremely* stressful state.

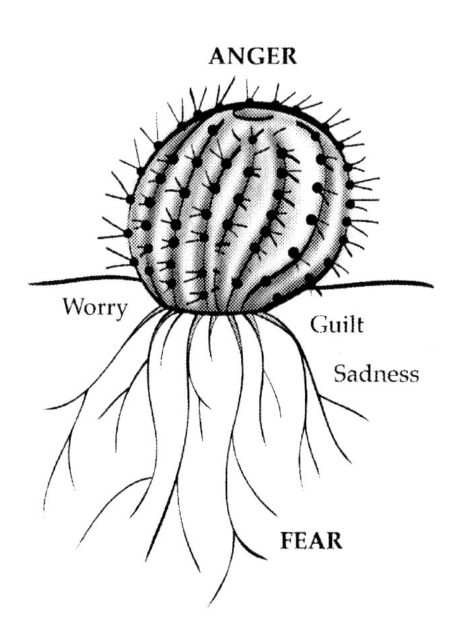

According to Stress Management Specialist, Dr. Naras Bhat, "A single episode of anger can suppress the immune system for up to six hours. At an atomic level, stress hormones *attack* the nucleus of cells and change the structure of DNA, resulting in immune disorders. The suppressed immune system can contribute to infections, allergies, cancer, or autoimmune disorders."

Sometimes it is easy to ignore vulnerable feelings like fear, worry, guilt, and sadness. If you are prone to protecting yourself from vulnerability, then hanging on to the anger may allow you to feel more "in control" and powerful. However, if you want to increase your E.Q., and lower your stress levels, you'll need to explore your anger *and* the underlying vulnerable feelings that are buried underneath.

Keep in mind, if your feelings are particularly strong, painful, or traumatic—then seek help from a qualified mental health professional before attempting to utilize this tool. Know that, when needed, professional support is an extremely worthwhile investment in your overall mind/body health. Take good care of yourself by reaching out for support.

If moving ahead feels appropriate to you, then use the following four-step tool to clarify your feelings and increase your emotional awareness/E.Q. As with any new skill that is being developed, you may feel awkward at first. And remember—if you keep practicing and flexing this important E.Q. muscle, then your emotional awareness will undoubtedly increase.

First read through the instructions. Then, put this tool into action by completing the journaling assignment at the end of the chapter.

♦♦♦♦♦♦♦♦♦♦♦♦♦♦♦♦♦♦♦♦♦♦♦♦♦♦♦

E.Q. Stress-Reduction Tool

Step 1: Sit upright in a comfortable chair. Prepare yourself to go inward by taking some nice, deep abdominal breaths.

Step 2: To enter a light meditative state, gently close your eyes and visualize yourself in a cozy, dimly lit environment.

Step 3: As you continue to take deep abdominal breaths, imagine that you are scanning your body from top to bottom for any tension points. While you're scanning yourself, picture a warm glow where any tightness, ache, or pain is residing. Without judgment, become aware of the intensity of each warm glow that you sense.

Now that you have scanned your physical landscape, it is time to tune into your emotional landscape. By doing so, you will be acknowledging stresses at both physical and emotional levels.

Step 4: To check in emotionally and look for stressful feelings, simply ask: "What's Buggin' Me?" Explore whatever emotions surface to see if you're holding any anger, fear, worry, guilt, or sadness. Process each feeling by journaling about your discoveries. If you find anger, process it first, then investigate below the surface. Since anger is a secondary emotion, keep in mind that moving below it will clarify what vulnerable feelings are lurking in the roots.

♦♦♦♦♦♦♦♦♦♦♦♦♦♦♦♦♦♦♦♦♦♦♦♦♦

One of my clients, Jim, was using this E.Q. Stress-Reduction Tool one night before going to sleep. After completing the initial steps, he began to journal about his closest friend who had been laid off. He wrote about three different emotions that he felt.

1. Anger toward the poor economy

2. Survivor's guilt because he had a job when his friend didn't

3. Sadness about not being able to work with his buddy anymore

Jim's description of his thoughts and feelings included some physical responses that he became aware of while he was writing. He noticed that he felt jaw tension when he tuned into his anger. He felt heaviness in his chest when he focused on his survivor's guilt. In addition, Jim experienced tightness in his throat when he connected with his sadness. He took some deep breaths to relax his throat and jaw. After breathing into the tension, more sadness came up.

Working with the four steps of the E.Q. Stress-Reduction Tool led Jim to a healthy exploration and release of his buried feelings. After going through this process, he felt more at peace and slept soundly that night.

JOURNALING:

1. Start with Step 1 of the E.Q. Stress-Reduction Tool. Follow the instructions for each step and move through the 4-step process. If your

emotions are at manageable levels, remember to explore them "above" and "below ground" to clear the various layers of stressful feelings.

Consider using this tool and writing in your journal on a daily basis. If time is scarce, then simply journal before going to sleep each night and prompt yourself by asking, "What's Buggin' Me?"

2. Complete this sentence through journaling:

What's clear to me now is...

Thoughts... Emotions... Memories... Sensations...

Inner Explorations and Inquiries...

Thoughts... Emotions... Memories... Sensations...

Inner Explorations and Inquiries...

Thoughts... Emotions... Memories... Sensations...

5

The Art of Listening

When it comes to internal communications, meditation is a powerful stress-reduction tool that helps us connect to our inner landscapes. After we become comfortable with meditating, it allows many of us to be with our innermost thoughts and feelings while *coming home* to the richness inside. For this reason, a daily meditation practice teaches us *the art of listening—to ourselves.*

So now that our *going-inward tool,* meditation, is in place—what about our abilities to go *outward* to connect? How can we build bridges that will emotionally connect us to one another? With depression on the rise today, it's obvious how isolated and lonely many people are feeling. Our frantically-paced days can leave us with frazzled nerves and a yearning to be seen, heard, and understood by another human being.

Larry Dossey, M.D., the author of *Space, Time & Medicine,* uses the term "hurry sickness" to describe people's over-concern for schedules, time, and the ongoing ticking-of-the-clock. This intense focus on external time can cause internal pressure to build. Dossey cites hurry sickness in the rise of stress-related problems, such as: heart disease, high blood pressure, and depression.

♦ ♦

I worked on *Reversing Stress and Burnout* for almost two years with author Naras Bhat, M.D., F.A.C.P. I became deeply engaged with the project as the creative director, editor, and illustrator. Working with all the exciting personal growth material, and already being a meditation teacher, made me start to think about making a shift in my career. After the *Reversing Stress and Burnout* book was published, I decided to go back to school and become a Certified Clinical Hypnotherapist. Doing so would allow me to be with people throughout the day, and not just work alone on a computer—this sounded wonderful!

And now that my training is complete, I am in private practice. I love going to my office and being fully present with clients. For me, it is a privilege to hold a sacred space for people's tender feelings and serve as a *Power Partner* while they move toward their goals. In addition to the educational and hypnotherapy tools I use, compassionate listening is also an important part of each session. As numerous therapists will attest, the art of listening is an important and useful *Life Tool.* And when you think about today's hustle and bustle—isn't receiving someone's full and undivided attention a *precious gift?*

As a kid, I remember feeling starved for positive attention. When my dad wasn't working day and night at the store he owned, he sat at home reading a newspaper—wrapped around him as if it were a shield or protective fortress. As a little girl, I would stand in front of this fortress and ask him something like, "Daddy, will you draw me a cat?" Or "Can we play checkers later?" Keep in mind that I would usually have to ask a question several times before he would s-l-o-w-l-y lower his *drawbridge*—even for a moment. On a day he felt generous, he would finally peer over the "wall" with furrowed eyebrows and an annoyed look—and say something like, "What do you want now?" Or maybe it was "*Who goes there?*"

When I was grown, my father admitted to me how incredibly uncomfortable and alone he had always felt—even in the presence of others. That was one of our most important conversations. I listened with heartfelt attention as he allowed me one short and honest glimpse behind his protective fortress. To this day, I am grateful for that one important connection to my unarmored father. Hopefully, now that Dad is on the other side, he has found a connection again…and for longer than a few brief moments.

♦ ♦

Active Listening: Three Simple Steps

Are you ready to study *the art of listening* now? I hope you will join me because I can't tell you how much my life changed after taking a lengthy training in effective communication skills. That training was one of my best investments. If you've already got healthy communication skills, that is wonderful. You can simply consider this chapter a review. Then, the next time you have an opportunity to connect deeply with someone—turn off the TV, your cell phone, the computer, and put down the newspaper, or your book. *Gift the person* with your glorious, undivided attention.

The art of listening, in various communication training methods is often called *Active Listening.* Active Listening is a focused way of receiving information from another. It is a three-step process that truly is active. By contrast, *passive listening* or robotically, "Uh-huhing…" as a form of listening contains little action and the communication is basically stuck on autopilot. Let's release the autopilot switch and mindfully connect. *Shall we?*

The three steps of Active Listening are *mirroring, validation,* and *empathy.* One of the keys to success here is to pull back your energy from sharing yourself, so you can be fully present for the person you are connecting with. In preparation, if you consciously deepen your breath into your belly it will help you get grounded. Then you can *receive* information from the other person more effectively.

When I teach Active Listening to clients, I use a prop to assist in the training. This prop is a basketball that I've written notes on—kind of like a big round "cheat sheet." When I introduce the client to this basketball, I often quip that "communication was never meant to be a competitive sport!"

In Native American traditions, when Indians are meeting in a circle, a *talking stick* is passed around to designate whose turn it is to speak. When someone is holding the talking stick, they can not be interrupted. That is the rule of respect. So picture the basketball or a talking stick, if you prefer, with the following prompts for the Active Listener carved onto its surface:

1. Mirroring: After the person you are listening to is finished sharing, reflect back what you have heard him or her say. This will let the person know you are fully present and listening. Paraphrase the person's content in your own language. You might begin with: *It sounds like…, I'm sensing that…, I hear that…, I see that…*

2. Validation: This requires listening for the feeling that is oftentimes underneath the content of his or her sharing. Mindfully hold back judgment or criticism during this step and simply validate the person's emotions. You might validate by saying: *I can see how…, it makes sense that…, I can understand why…*

3. Empathy: Consider what it would be like to step into and walk in the moccasins of the other person. Be aware of your bodily reactions to what is being shared. This will give you more information and empathy toward what he or she has been through. When it feels appropriate, you might even share this reaction with the person you are listening to.

For example, Jill is telling her friend—the Active Listener—about almost having an accident on the freeway. Here is their conversation:

♦♦♦♦♦♦♦♦♦♦♦♦♦♦♦♦♦♦♦♦♦♦♦

Jill: "Whew, I had a close call on the freeway today. A red convertible abruptly cut in front of me. I slammed on my brakes, swerved a bit, and barely missed hitting it! My heart was pounding so hard afterwards that I could barely catch my breath."

Active Listener *mirroring:* "Wow, <u>sounds like</u> you came very close to having an accident."

Jill: "You got that right! It took me a while to calm my racing heart down afterward."

Active Listener *validating:* "<u>I can see why</u> your heart was racing—that's scary to have such a close call."

Jill: "Yeah, I'm lucky I wasn't fiddling with the radio or my cell phone when the person cut me off. If I hadn't been paying full attention it could've been a major collision."

Active Listener *empathizing:* "Just hearing you share about this near accident makes my stomach tense up. I'm so glad you were paying attention to the road when the convertible cut you off."

Jill: "Me too! Thanks for letting me get this off my chest. It really helps to have your support."

♦♦♦♦♦♦♦♦♦♦♦♦♦♦♦♦♦♦♦♦♦♦♦

Can you see why Jill felt deeply heard and supported in this conversation? Her friend, the Active Listener, didn't cut her sharing short by launching into a drama about *his* own auto accident ten years ago. He chose to contain his response in order to support and nurture her feelings. And keep in mind, with the fast-paced nature of many conversations—it can take practice to contain our responses and not eagerly want to *grab the talking stick!*

The art of listening is an opportunity for you to do your best to see, hear, and understand the person you are connecting with. Let go of as many preconceived ideas and judgments about this person as you possibly can. And, don't interrupt while they are sharing—let them have your full attention.

Finally, Active Listening is a wonderful gift that you can offer others to help them feel deeply connected. And connectedness has been clinically shown to be a stress reducer—which is great for your health!

JOURNALING:

1. Meditate for a moment about what you have read regarding *the art of listening.* Journal about what comes up for you. Do you have any resistance to actively listening to others in a deep way?

2. Set a realistic goal for yourself to practice Active Listening for the upcoming week. Would a few times a week, or once a day, feel appropriate to practice? In order to have a practice partner, is there someone with whom you can share this chapter?

Write your communication goals in this journal and check off your progress. When completed, feel free to add your accomplishments to Chapter 14: Victories!

3. Complete this sentence through journaling:

What's clear to me now is…

Inner Explorations and Inquiries...

Thoughts... Emotions... Memories... Sensations...

Inner Explorations and Inquiries...

Thoughts… Emotions… Memories… Sensations…

Inner Explorations and Inquiries...

Thoughts... Emotions... Memories... Sensations...

6

Oops—Triangulation on Board

Now that you have been practicing *the art of listening*, how about bringing your attention to another aspect of communication? This chapter is about identifying and breaking habits of indirect communication.

Unfortunately, sharing vulnerabilities is not often a skill handed down from one generation to the next. Instead, what is commonly handed down is a major barrier to healthy communication: triangulation. As the word implies, triangulation happens when communication is indirect, behind someone's back, and involves three people. Triangulation becomes an over-used form of communication when someone lacks the awareness or skill to directly communicate his or her *feelings and needs* to another person. In this way, triangulation becomes the opposite of one-to-one talk.

Honest communication requires great courage. And, as you have undoubtedly noticed—speaking your truth with a loved one is no easy endeavor. Getting up the nerve to have a revealing one-to-one talk is *stressful.* Preparing to have "the talk" can take days or even weeks—that is *if* fear doesn't prompt you to abandon the idea.

One reason for not pursuing a needed one-to-one talk is a fear that doing so will end the relationship. Or, you may simply be afraid that you will hurt the other person's feelings. Although these reasons may or may not have some validity, the danger is that when you repeatedly avoid the important one-to-one talks, the resentments may add up and eventually cause a decline in the quality of the relationship. If you don't speak your truth to a loved one, you may be hiding important parts of yourself from that relationship.

For example, in the Williams family triangulation was a mainstay of the family diet. Jim and Dorothy Williams had two grown children, John and Beth. One continual communication triangle in this family was between mom (Dorothy), John, and Beth. A triangle recently became activated when Beth and John made plans to attend a concert featuring classical music. As it turned out, John canceled at the last minute and went to a sporting event with a buddy.

Instead of having a *heart-to-heart* talk with John, Beth used mom to vent. After listening to her anger and frustration, mom took on Beth's feelings, called John, and gave him "a piece of her mind." Or was it a piece of *Beth's mind?*

John's defensive reaction to mom was to blame Beth. "Beth knows I don't like classical music yet she bought the concert tickets without asking me first. I didn't want to go from the start, but went along with it to try to be a 'good guy.' Then this really fun opportunity came along—and I couldn't resist."

Hurt and disappointed, Beth withdrew from John and missed an opportunity to honestly tell him how his behavior affected her. Feeling blamed and misunderstood, John also withdrew from Beth. He too missed an opportunity to let her know that he would like to be invited to an event before the tickets are bought. That way, he could let her know if he was interested in the event or not.

Why People Triangulate

You may wonder why anyone would triangulate since it is such a barrier to healthy communication. Obviously, there are a few payoffs or none of us would indulge in it. One payoff is a momentary feeling of closeness to the person we are triangulating with (at the expense of the person being talked about). For example, Beth and mom felt momentary closeness when they were "on the same side" against John. But, by choosing this method to feel close, they each missed healthier ways to connect with each other—and with John.

The second payoff for triangulating is that "blowing off steam" toward the third party of the triangle momentarily lowers anxiety. Unfortunately though, these payoffs come at the expense of working out issues directly with loved ones and end up blocking healthy, direct relating. The triangulating process offers *short-term gains* that often create *long-term pains* by blocking honest emotional intimacy.

Stress-Reducing Tool: Healthy, Direct Communication

If, after reading this chapter, Mom (Dorothy) decides to disengage from triangulation and use healthy communication skills with her family, she could alternatively:

- Not "take on" Beth's and John's emotions and stay neutral. Since triangles thrive on high emotions and anxiety, a calm response doesn't escalate situations.
- Identify her own feelings with family members and ask for *heart-to-heart talks* with each person involved.
- Suggest that Beth and John honestly talk to one another about their issue. She could tell them that healing the upset may come from taking turns attentively listening to one another—not in an attempt to be right, but as a way to step into the other's shoes.
- Bring the focus back to showing interest in Beth (or whomever she is talking with). She may assertively say something like: "Beth, I know you and John can work things out between yourselves and since our time to visit is limited, I'd like to hear more about your…"

Positive Payoffs for Letting Go of Triangulation

- Allows more authenticity into your relationships
- Encourages direct relating so you can get to know others better, as well as give others an opportunity to know you better
- Increases healthy connectedness, which lowers stress

Finally, by trading in triangulation for a compassionate, assertive communication style, we will all be courageously choosing to increase the amount of authenticity in our lives.

JOURNALING:

So, now that you have a better understanding of triangulation, how about doing some self-inquiry to see if triangulating has crept into your communication repertoire with loved ones? Are you willing to consider some of Dorothy's new *stress-busting methods* of disengaging from triangulation in order to increase your direct connections with others?

1. Take a few minutes and explore this question through meditation: Are there any recurring communication triangles in your life? If so, journal about the example that comes into your mind. Explore any feelings you felt at the time while triangulating or that you feel in this moment. Write about the feelings.

2. Meditate for a few minutes and connect with your Inner Consultant to get constructive feedback on what could be a healthier way to deal with triangulation issues in the future. Rewrite your example now and, if needed, refer back to the healthy suggestions offered earlier in this chapter. Now take a few minutes to meditate and imagine this new, healthier scenario in your mind's eye.

3. Complete this sentence through journaling:

What's clear to me now is…

Thoughts... Emotions... Memories... Sensations...

Inner Explorations and Inquiries...

Thoughts... Emotions... Memories... Sensations...

Inner Explorations and Inquiries…

Thoughts... Emotions... Memories... Sensations...

7

Soft Eyes

Becoming deeply acquainted with oneself is no small task. For this reason, connecting to one's inner workings is an ongoing, ever changing, and lifelong process. What makes this endeavor a slow but rich experience is that the essence of oneself may be buried under many layers of the personality. Therefore, getting past the encrusted layers to connect with the precious, authentic core can be quite an excavation process.

Similar to a real geological excavation, chipping away at your outer (hardened) rock formations to get to the gold beneath can take incredible perseverance and patience. For this reason, it helps to not make the journey alone. Having the support of fellow seekers and a therapeutic guide may inspire a more productive and fulfilling excavation.

Another gift of having other *hands to hold* is that if your own flashlight becomes dim and tired, the light from companion seekers can help you navigate until you feel recharged. In addition, having the love and support from others can assist you in finding compassion for some of the parts you may discover directly under the surface. For example, you may react with harsh judgment when you face shadowy, previously buried parts of your self for the first time. For this reason, seeing through another's empathic eyes can be a wonderful help until you find your own *soft eyes.*

For me, letting go of harsh judgments toward some of the vulnerable, "less-than-perfect" parts of myself is an ongoing process requiring periodic updates. To see myself (darks, lights, and grays) through compassionate, loving eyes, I find that first I need to identify, and then remove, my judgmental glasses.

This process allowed me to see that the *prescription glasses* through which I harshly viewed myself, dated back to early childhood. These distorted lenses belonged to people who were projecting their pain and frustrations onto me. Even though these glasses were clearly outdated, I carted them around because I believed that they were accurate. It was painful to realize I had unconsciously kept renewing the prescription for these incredibly distorted glasses—year after year.

By no coincidence, a rich experience came my way that increased my ability to look upon *all* of myself more compassionately. It happened while I was attending a daylong workshop about speaking from the Authentic Self. The purpose of this seminar was to create a safe container from which to access one's authentic voice and share it with others.

In preparation for the first exercise, the workshop facilitator paired us up with someone we didn't know. We were asked to face each other, gently hold our partner's hands, and then take turns speaking from our hearts. As you might imagine, this was initially quite scary. However, as the day went on, defenses melted and many people began to truly enjoy the experience. Laughter could be heard throughout the room. Many of the participants discovered that hearing others and being heard by soulful, safe strangers could feel quite wonderful.

For the final exercise of the day, our facilitator asked us not to speak at all, but just hold a partner's hands and experience being authentic without words. "Let the body and the eyes do the speaking this time," he suggested.

I was paired with a fellow in his mid-forties named Anthony. His arms and hands appeared deformed. I nervously began thinking about how Anthony must be struggling with this new version of the exercise. A heavy sadness filled my chest as I looked at his hands and connected with parts of myself that sometimes feel different from, and *less than,* others. Shame began bubbling up from the center of my being. Thank God this painful spiral was interrupted when the facilitator signaled for us to begin.

Anthony reached toward me first and offered his warm, misshapen fingers. As I reached back and looked into his eyes, I saw a loving, compassionate confidence I had *never* seen before—*from anyone.* He extended his fingers with such exquisite grace that I, too, was able to experience and feel their beauty. Clearly, Anthony was much more at peace in his own skin than I was in mine.

This realization sent a wave of sadness through me. I breathed into my vulnerability while continuing to look into Anthony's gentle blue eyes. The pale blue reminded me of a quiet pool of water—a still and smooth surface, yet deep. As I continued gazing, my sad feelings gently began to melt and the muscles around my eyes started to relax. Anthony and I smiled at one another. It was then, in that sacred moment, that I joined him in the precious silence of *simply being.*

Graciously, Anthony shared his authentic core with me. He turned his flashlight in my direction and modeled compassionate, confident self-love. Anthony was a fellow excavator offering me a priceless gift. What a soulful blessing I received—a truly radiant experience!

Since then, whenever I am struggling and finding it difficult to see another or myself compassionately, I simply tap into *seeing through Anthony's loving eyes.* That immediately softens my vision and warms my heart.

JOURNALING:

This exercise is one of peering below your Topsoil. Letting go of seeing your shadowy or vulnerable sides through harsh eyes can be a powerful first step toward finding your own *soft eyes.* For this reason, it may be time to assess how old your visual lenses are. (Wouldn't it be wonderful if LensCrafters sent out periodic postcards reminding us to have our *inner vision* checked?)

1. Are you ready to practice seeing yourself (the shadowy or vulnerable sides) through compassionate eyes? If so, then meditate for a moment and come up with something about yourself—a personality trait or a physical feature—that you struggle with. Identify what situations often trigger the inner struggle. Journal about what comes up for you.

2. Now think about someone who has looked at you in a compassionate, nonjudgmental, and loving way. Try to remember the look in their eyes and imagine yourself looking back at them. Can you let in the person's *soft eyes* regarding the issue that you identified in # 1? Meditate on this for a few minutes. Notice how your body (particularly your heart) feels when you think about this. Gently breathe into this experience and allow it to nurture you.

3. Know that the reward of this deeply fulfilling *re-visioning work* is lovingly learning to see yourself through your own soft eyes. Here are several soulful

questions that may inspire you to continue peering below your Topsoil. Think about the questions, and then add your responses to this journal:

- When I look at myself through harsh eyes, whose prescription glasses am I annually having refilled?
- Am I willing to take off any outdated lenses I have been wearing and be open to seeing myself through my own *soft eyes?* (Or, if you prefer: Am I open to seeing myself through Anthony's eyes?)
- Knowing I will continually grow and change, can I love and accept all of me (darks, lights, and grays) in this moment?

Several people who worked with this material said they were surprised to receive more clarity about where or who some of their own harsh self-judgments were coming from. They even imagined taking off the negative glasses and returning them to their original owners.

4. Complete this sentence through journaling:

What's clear to me now is…

Thoughts… Emotions… Memories… Sensations…

Inner Explorations and Inquiries...

Thoughts... Emotions... Memories... Sensations...

Inner Explorations and Inquiries...

Thoughts... Emotions... Memories... Sensations...

8

Soul Nourishment

Before we get to the heart of this chapter, let's do a little guided imagery for a minute. Relax into the chair or cushion you are sitting on and allow your breathing to sink into your belly. Close your eyes and imagine a yellow balloon lying on the ground in front of you. As you look closer, you notice that the yellow balloon hasn't had any air blown into it—this airless balloon is completely empty. Upon further examination you see that there is not a bit of lightness or bounce in this poor balloon's life!

Now imagine reaching down and picking up the empty yellow balloon. Sense yourself blowing air into it and hear the sounds coming from your throat as you do so. Through your *life-giving breath,* the yellow balloon grows larger and expands. You feel its lightness increasing as it gently opens your hands farther apart with every breath. When the fullness, roundness, and plumpness of the yellow balloon feel complete, you gently knot its end. As you toss it playfully into the air, you see that your breath has filled this once empty balloon and gifted it with a lightness of being.

Slowly open your eyes when you are ready and bring your awareness back to the environment you're in.

I often use this imagery with clients. That is why I keep an airless yellow balloon in my office cabinet. I shared this guided imagery recently, after one of my clients, Andrea, was talking about her deep yearning to be creative. She felt she had no talent because her younger sister was "the artist" in their family. After the imagery, I gently placed the airless yellow balloon onto the empty chair next to her and explained that her creativity was just like this balloon. The container was there for it—in fact fully formed and waiting—it was simply that she had never given her creativity a single *life-giving breath* to propel its form into motion. Andrea's eyes began to fill with tears as she opened to the idea that maybe she could explore her own creativity...and embrace her heart's desire.

So, hopefully, by doing the upcoming exercise in this chapter, you'll be encouraged to mindfully put your life-giving breath into your heart's desires. By doing this regularly, you will be nourishing your soul on an ongoing basis—thus expanding your personal fulfillment while reducing stress! And, just so you notice, expanding (like the balloon) is the key word here. Expansion is equated with relaxing and opening; whereas contraction, the opposite feeling, is what many of us feel after a hectic day when our muscles tense in response to a multitude of stressors.

As an example of countering stressful contraction, have you noticed how relaxed and open you feel after you have spent the day doing an activity that is *Soul Food* for you? At the end of the day you probably experienced a satisfied and expanded feeling. One of my clients, Jeff, describes how he feels while he is hiking in nature with his wife. He says, "Being with the earth, trees, and the relaxed conversation—transforms me into one happy and carefree soul!"

When I begin to share this stress-reducing tool in workshops, participants are asked to make a list of Soul Foods that nourish their hearts. These are activities and *no actual foods* are allowed on the lists. The reason for this is that too many of us *use food* to habitually self-soothe. This tool helps us expand "our tastes" beyond food.

One of the best parts of this activity is hearing people's unique, yet, sincere responses. The secondary gift is watching people add additional Soul Foods to their own plates—after they have listened to what other folks have said. A smorgasbord of Soul Foods literally begins to form, which allows everyone to share their favorites!

When people add to their lists it suggests that either they were reminded of some Soul Food they forgot to write down—or they decided to sample (and taste) others' favorites. For whichever reason, the exciting part is watching the participants' lists *grow!*

Now, before reading the compiled list of other people's responses to this exercise, take some deep belly breaths. Get centered in meditation for a few minutes and then ask yourself the upcoming question (have a pen handy). Allow yourself to answer the question over and over again in your mind, exploring it from numerous directions.

"What is it in my life today that nourishes
my heart's desires and feels like *Soul Food?*"

Journal about what comes through for you on the lined pages at the end of this chapter. By the way, scribbles and doodles are highly encouraged. And, if it helps, revisit some of the most joyful, heartfelt moments from your past. Then ask yourself, "What was the essence, or core, of those moments that nourished my soul?" Know that laughing and crying can be a part of this process. When you have pondered every angle you can think of, return to reading this chapter.

How did you do? Were you able to list various experiences and activities that are soulfully nourishing? To further assist you on this inquiry, here is a list of simplified responses (in no particular order) to the Soul Nourishment Exercise from my workshop participants. Hopefully, you will consider adding some of these to your list—if they resonate with your heart's desires—and you've not already written them down. Let's see which of these *whet your soulful appetite:*

Connecting with loved ones
Nurturing a child
Walking mindfully in nature
Doing work that makes a difference in the world (either volunteer or paid)
Looking in the mirror and seeing love in your own eyes
Listening to uplifting music
Taking turns reading to one another
Enjoying the exquisite scent of a favorite candle
Feeling spiritually connected
Making love with your partner
Stroking a canvas with a paint-loaded brush
Accepting your aging process with grace, humor, and self-love
Giving and receiving back massages
Praying
Curling up with a great book
Performing in front of an audience
Meditating
Writing from your heart

Feeling the warmth of a camp fire

Playing Scrabble

Lying on a beach with the sand cradling every inch of you

Exercising and playing sports with others

Running your hands slowly over silk

Speaking your truth

Giving to a friend in need

Feeling the sun on your face and the wind in your hair

Receiving from a friend—when you are in need

Traveling to inspiring places

Connecting with people who feel emotionally safe (and then letting them see both your strengths and vulnerabilities)

Dancing with joyful abandon

Laughing hysterically with a friend until you both practically *wet your britches!*

Planting a garden/playing in the dirt

Enjoying heartfelt conversations: feeling seen, heard, and understood

Cuddling a pet

Hanging out in a bookstore for hours on a rainy day

Finding your flock

Watching a favorite film with a good friend

Running

Helping/serving others

Turning off the TV and telling stories with loved ones

Being internally comfortable with yourself and savoring quiet time alone—without outward distractions

Is there anything from this list that you feel inspired to add or process through your journaling? Keep in mind that heart's desires are as unique as every individual on this planet. For this reason, what *has heart* for one person may *induce sleep* in another. Only the heart pumping in each chest truly knows what it needs to feel positively fed and soulfully nourished.

Also keep in mind that when a heart has its deepest desires suppressed, it may be contracted and longing for fulfillment. If this feels true for you, then consider giving yourself permission to nurture your heart in healthy, soulful ways—each and every day.

Let's face it—there is no need to skimp when it comes to *juicy activities* that nourish your heart's desires. In fact, if it feels right, share your Soul Food list with a loved one and see if they will reciprocate by making a list to share with you—thus providing a "second helping" and possibly some shared soulful activities!

JOURNALING:

1. For the upcoming week, at the end of each of your daily meditations, ask yourself:

"What is one thing I could do today that would nurture my heart?"

For instance, you may become inspired to bring fresh flowers into the office or take a bagged lunch and eat at the park. Simple requests that come from within can be Soul Food. So take time to listen to your heart's desires each day. *You will be nourishing yourself from the inside out and countering stress.*

2. Look over your Soul Food list and choose several activities that are calling to you. Schedule the solo activities into your calendar. For some activities with others, pick up the phone and schedule some *Soulful Play Dates.*

3. Complete this sentence through journaling:

What's clear to me now is…

Inner Explorations and Inquiries...

Thoughts... Emotions... Memories... Sensations...

Inner Explorations and Inquiries...

Thoughts… Emotions… Memories… Sensations…

Inner Explorations and Inquiries…

Thoughts... Emotions... Memories... Sensations...

9

Undesirable Urges

We all have undesirable urges that creep into our days. Some we notice and choose not to indulge in, while others get the best of us. Let's face it, temptations are often all around, but for a variety of reasons our willpower may fluctuate.

In my private practice, clients come in with various habits they want to overcome. These habits include: smoking, fingernail biting, teeth grinding, and the most popular challenge—overeating. Let's focus on the overeating issue for a few minutes.

I recently heard a woman say that her two best friends were food and a good book. She went on to explain that food is the only thing she can count on 24 hours a day for unconditional love. Another woman shared that food is control for her, a device to push down anxiety, anger, and sadness. Eating to fill feelings of emptiness and loneliness is a common problem. When food is one of our closest friends, it often becomes a foe when we look in the mirror.

I have used food, and especially sweets, in an attempt to *self-soothe.* My extremely painful childhood left me chronically yearning for comfort, sweetness, security, love, and safety. One of the few happy memories from my childhood occurred on Sunday afternoons. Our family would go to Dunkin' Donuts and buy a colorful "variety pack." A dozen donuts: regular, cake, and glazed. When we would get home, one of my parents would make coffee, and then we would break open the glorious box of donuts.

Dipping these treats in hot coffee was a major pleasure for me! I'd savor the coffee-soaked donuts and be transported into a momentary fantasy of seeing us as a unified and happy family. This was *bliss!* As fleeting as it was, I felt safe, secure, and loved. Unfortunately, seeking those warm, sweet feelings became an ongoing quest in my eating life for many years thereafter.

As a teenager and young adult, when I felt lonely or worried about something I would crave sweets—especially donuts. If I gave in to the craving, a desperate feeling fueled my eating. I urgently tried to re-experience emotional connectedness. I would savor each bite and then rush to the next one. It felt as though love was *almost* within my reach, *and if I didn't hurry—I'd miss it.* Thankfully, at twenty-nine, I stepped onto a personal growth path that would change my life, including my relationship with food. I found healthier ways to deal with my hunger for love. Unfortunately, as many of us have experienced, the problem with using food (or drugs or alcohol) in an attempt to fill our inner voids is that it simply doesn't accomplish what our souls are starving for—be it safety, acceptance, respect, validation, security, companionship, or love.

Although our habits can't fill the *holes-in-our-souls,* they do serve us on some levels (even unhealthy habits). For this reason, create a safe container for your personal growth work. When you are ready to let go of behaviors/habits that are not serving your highest good or health, no matter what the goal, take care of yourself by getting plenty of support.

If your goal is to free yourself from a drug or alcohol addiction—immediately contact a qualified mental health professional. Talk with your medical doctor and an addiction specialist. You deserve experienced guidance and support. Similarly, if you choose to quit smoking, consult your medical doctor before actually stopping. Prior planning will increase the likelihood that you will successfully achieve your goals.

When Jennifer first came to see me she had an enormous *Inner Critic* who loved tormenting her about her compulsive eating habits and her body size. Through our work together, she was able to "dis-identify" from her Inner Critic and find out what Core Beliefs and fears were fueling her overeating. After Jennifer began taming her Inner Critic she uncovered a compassionate, self-loving part inside. Having this supportive *Inner Cheerleader* is truly a gift to her life today. What's more, when her Inner Critic stopped *stealing the spotlight,* she began noticing that her rebellious eating habits naturally started to quiet down. Jennifer consequently increased her personal power by making more conscious choices, including losing her excess weight.

One of the first steps I take with a client who wants to break an unhealthy habit is to request that the two of us team up and become detectives. Together, we look for clues that will clarify what is *really* going on. We start with the unwanted habit (smoking, fingernail biting, overeating, etc.) and then trace it backwards.

For example, Tom came to see me because he wanted to stop biting his fingernails. After we became acquainted, I asked him to make a list of benefits he would receive if he stopped biting his nails.

He wrote: "No longer feel bad about how my nails look, no need to hide my hands in my pockets, and no embarrassment while holding my wife's hand across the table in a restaurant."

"Great reasons to quit!" I enthused. "Can you think of some people who will be supportive of your quitting?"

"My wife would love for me to quit. And my mom would be happy about it too. They will both support me for sure."

"Wonderful," I said. "Support is important when any of us are making personal changes. Now let's get to our detective work. Can you remember what was going on in your life when you first started biting your nails?"

Tom rubbed his index finger across his bottom lip. His eyes narrowed as he methodically searched for an answer. "I was about twelve when I fractured my ankle during a soccer game. Lying in bed with a cast around my leg was brutal. All I could think about was how many games I would have to miss! I blamed myself for not being a better athlete. That's when I started feeling really anxious. I had too much time to lie there and think. I was angry and bored out of my mind waiting for my ankle to heal. The next thing I knew, I was chewing my nails to the quick."

"What a frustrating situation! That must've been so tough having to wait while your ankle healed," I sighed. "I'm glad you remembered what first triggered the biting, that will help us understand this habit."

Next, I asked Tom to think about the last time that he was chewing his nails. He recalled an episode earlier that day. "What was happening before you started chewing your nails today?" I inquired.

"I usually start biting my nails when I'm alone in my office; I need privacy to indulge in this habit."

Earlier that day he was working on a demanding deadline when the habitual chewing started. "Can you tell me more?" I asked.

"I was sitting at my desk, thinking about everything I needed to do, when I started chewing my nails."

"And what were you *feeling* while thinking about everything you needed to do?" I asked.

"I remember feeling overwhelmed and anxious."

"Ahhh…good insight! Anything below the overwhelm and anxiety?"

"Fear," he replied with a quiver in his voice.

"Fear of what?"

"Fear of losing my job. The truth is, *I feel totally inadequate.*"

The energy in the room suddenly dropped. The covers were now pulled off of this Core Belief. The belief sat exposed between us. Our eyes were momentarily locked in silence. Finally, I repeated, "You feel totally inadequate?" For the next half-hour, Tom processed his sadness and vulnerability about this negative belief.

When he felt complete, I went to my wipe-off board. With a felt-tipped pen in hand, I began diagramming the chain of events that led to Tom's nail biting. I started drawing in the middle and worked backwards. I ended up with this diagram:

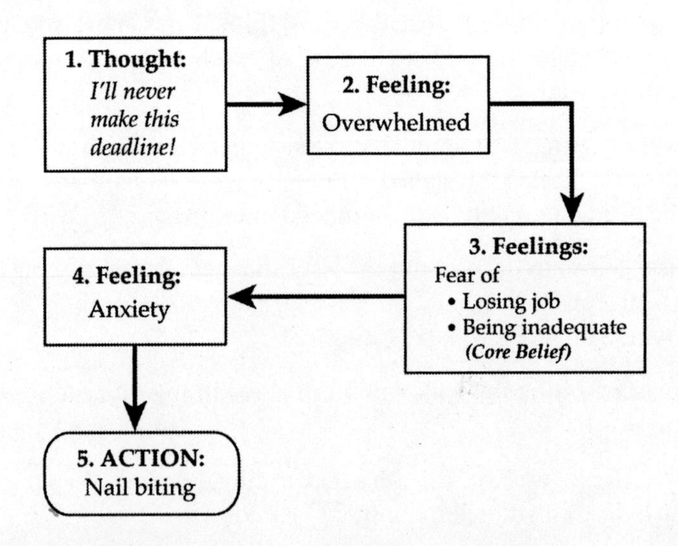

"Any thoughts or feelings after the nail biting?" I asked, still in my detective mode.

"Guilt. When I look at my chewed nails I feel revolted by what I've done." With a shameful look in his eyes, he said, "A couple of my cuticles were even bleeding from my self-mutilation." A few tears welled up as he embraced the deep feelings he had been avoiding.

After we talked about his emotional pain, I gently asked, "Then what?"

"I feel angry and inadequate—just like when I broke my ankle at twelve-years old!"

"Are the puzzle pieces coming together?" I asked.

I added these additional feelings to the diagram:

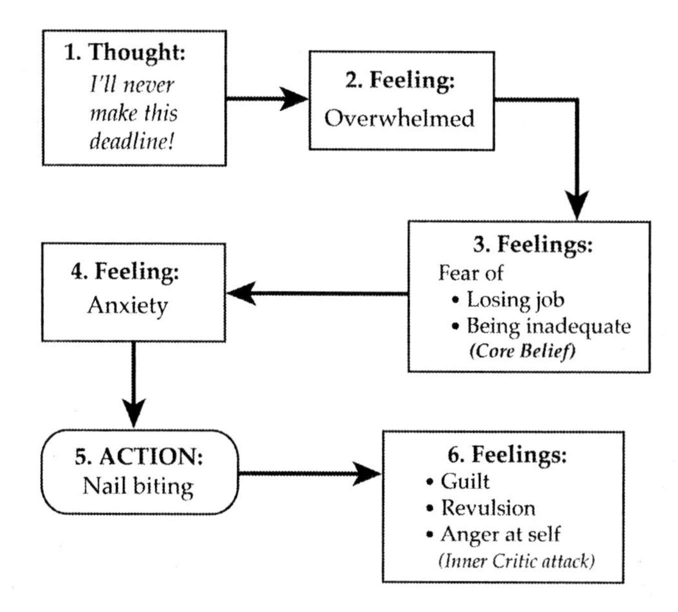

Through this diagramming, Tom and I were able to create a map of his nail-biting process by investigating the triggers that prompted the chain of events. And similar to any journey, when the map is not getting us to where we think it might—then it is time to acquire new resources and re-plot the course. After clarifying Tom's chain of events, we re-routed his map.

As for new resources, Tom and I explored his Core Belief—the feeling of inadequacy. When we first started processing this negative belief, I asked him to estimate how true this belief felt on a scale from 0 to 10. "Zero represents no truth to the belief, whereas 10 is 100% true."

"The belief feels like a 10." Tom replied.

"Do you feel the belief that you're *inadequate*, in any *particular place* in your body?" I asked.

Pointing to his solar plexus, he said, "I have a tight feeling here."

"Uh huh," I responded, shaking my head. "Now Tom, would you explain to me how you got to the high level position you currently hold with this company? Did you kidnap the guy who had your job—and you've been impersonating him for the last five years?" I asked playfully.

Tom laughed and then said, "I actually did well in school and I got my MBA from a high-powered, prestigious university. A successful interview, combined with my great education, helped me get hired. Then through perseverance and hard work, I moved my way up to this present position."

"So it sounds like you're completely qualified to handle this position and that you have earned it through schooling combined with dedicated hard work?" I listed these facts on the board.

He slowly began to nod his head.

"And how have your performance reviews gone?" I asked.

"I've always gotten rave reviews. Now that I think of it, I guess I'm the only person who doesn't believe I'm adequate."

"Tom," I said gently, "what you have been experiencing is called 'emotional reasoning.' Because your feelings of inadequacy are so *incredibly strong*, you believe them completely. The emotional side of you says: 'this feels 100% true, so it *must be true*.'"

After we engaged the left/logical side of his brain, Tom began to hear his emotional reasoning about feeling inadequate. Returning to the facts again poked holes in his Core Belief and weakened its grip.

We discussed how these feelings of inadequacy first came up after the soccer accident. With my guidance, he spent some time letting his nurturing "adult self" dialogue with the disappointed "inner twelve-year old" who still carried the shame from the accident. Tom learned how to *self-soothe* that day. In the process, he let the young boy inside know that it was *not* his fault. He explained to the "little guy" that even professional athletes get injured in games. This loving, compassionate reasoning was the same type of response he offered his son, Ricky, whenever he was struggling with a problem.

Tom began to release the emotional burden that he had carried since he was twelve. As I let the poignancy of the moment warm my heart, I was reminded why I deeply love this work.

"Now how true, from 0 to 10, is your belief about being inadequate?" I asked as I segued back into my detective mode.

Tom furrowed his eyebrows as he thought about the question from a logical perspective. He stared at the evidence I had written on the board. "About a 2," he beamed as he declared "and getting smaller every moment!"

"Excellent!" I cheered and enthusiastically clapped my hands together. "How's your solar plexus feeling now?"

He smiled, took a deep breath, and with relief in his voice said, "It's starting to relax."

After shining light on the chain of events that occurred both before and after the nail biting, Tom was no longer unconscious to his emotions and actions. His revised course included alternate thoughts and behaviors he could choose, when he became triggered by overwhelm or fear, instead of nail biting. Here is Tom's final diagram:

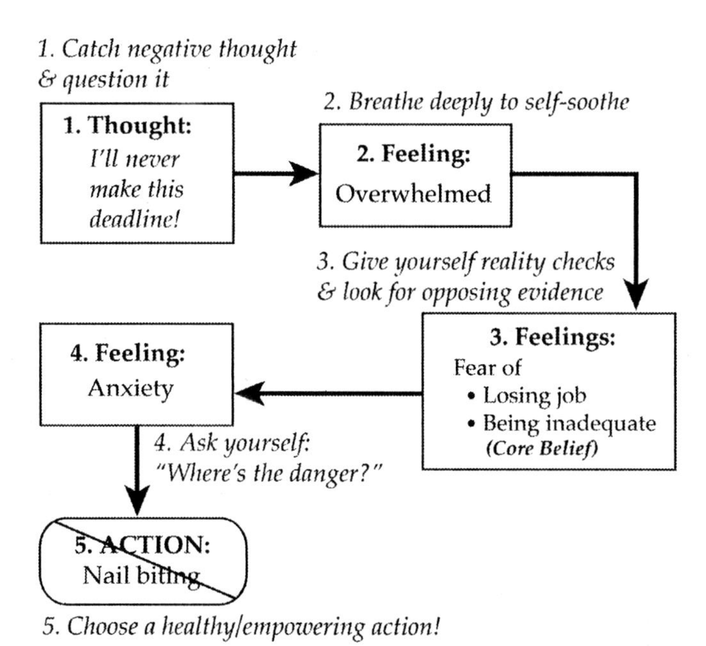

In addition to questioning his emotionally charged beliefs, Tom practiced belly breathing to lower his anxiety. When stressed, he also self-soothed by slowing down and taking one simple step at a time. When we were through, he had dealt with his unhealthy habit from various levels of mind and body. Today Tom is no longer a nail biter. He is *proud* of his healthy-looking hands. His wife is thrilled that he *kicked the habit!*

So whether you would like to stop biting your fingernails, smoking, or overeating, consider taking out your detective's magnifying glass to mindfully uncover your own chain of events. The methods shared here are empowering tools that can assist you in reaching your goals.

JOURNALING:

1. Become centered, belly breathe, and choose an unhealthy habit you would like to break.

Make a list of:

- Benefits you will receive by stopping this unhealthy habit
- Healthy rewards you will "gift yourself" with as you progress toward your goal
- Everyone you will invite into your support system while moving toward your goal; this includes appropriate medical professionals, family members, and friends

2. Think back to the last time that you gave in to the undesired behavior. Meditate for a few minutes on this issue and then journal to diagram/map out the chain of events. Remember to include thoughts, feelings, body sensations, and any Core Beliefs you uncover. Start with the unwanted habit and work backwards. See if you can trace the habit back to when it *first started.*

Next, fill in the feelings you experience after indulging in the unhealthy habit. Look for signs of emotional reasoning and counter these beliefs with logical thinking. Write your process down as it unfolds.

3. Add all of your accomplishments, both small and large, to Chapter 14: Victories! *(Know that I am applauding you here!)*

4. Complete this sentence through journaling:

What's clear to me now is…

Bonus Idea:
A Weight-Loss Journal for Eating Urges

If one of your goals is to lose weight, then you may want to have a separate journal for this purpose. For example, you can title the weight-loss journal something like, "Eating Urges," or, "Here's the Skinny." Then, each time *you crave unhealthy foods or overeat,* write an entry in your weight loss journal. You can answer and explore these *Important Inquisitive Questions:*

1. When did you have a craving for unhealthy foods or overeat? (Ex: Date and time of day)
2. Where? (Ex: At home, at work, or in your car)
3. Who were you with? (Or were you alone?)
4. What?

   a) What item/s you craved? (Ex: Chocolate chip cookies, French fries, etc.)

   b) What emotions you felt before eating? (Ex: Lonely, sad, angry, etc.)

   If you *gave in to the craving,* then answer these questions:

   c) What item/s you ate? (Ex: Chocolate chip cookies, French fries, etc.)

   d) What emotions you felt after eating? (Ex: Guilty, sad, etc.)

   e) What bodily sensations you felt after eating? (Ex: Bloated, gassy, etc.)

After you follow this format for a few days, you will probably discover some patterns. List the vulnerable times, places, and circumstances that you determine trigger your overeating. Check in with your Inner Consultant and journal about what options you can choose to *interrupt* your unhealthy cravings and overeating patterns. Finally, write down several healthy ways you can *nurture yourself* to celebrate your victories when you successfully interrupt your unhealthy eating patterns.

Inner Explorations and Inquiries...

Thoughts... Emotions... Memories... Sensations...

Inner Explorations and Inquiries...

Thoughts... Emotions... Memories... Sensations...

Inner Explorations and Inquiries...

Thoughts... Emotions... Memories... Sensations...

10

Letter for Release

Have you ever held a strong emotion inside for an extended period of time and then experienced the great relief that comes after talking to a close friend or therapist about it? You may have heard the saying, "We are only as sick as our secrets." In addition to verbally releasing emotions with someone you trust, letter writing can be an effective stress-reducing tool. Bringing unfinished business into the light through writing can be a great way to clarify, and then release your thoughts and feelings in a concrete way.

The key here is that when you decide to use this tool, you know from the moment you pick up the pen, that you will *not* mail this Letter for Release. This letter is simply meant to express raw, strong, maybe even irrational feelings that will be released from your gut and onto the paper. Then these highly-charged feelings can be seen, acknowledged, nurtured, released, and hopefully healed.

The Letters for Release that I've written for my personal growth have often been dramatic, no-holds-barred writing—a cathartic form of releasing. I would rant and rave about how hurt, disappointed, or angry I was, which usually led to a good cry in the purging process. Having gone through the full cycle of emotions I would feel cleansed and freer afterwards. This purging process is similar to a dramatic storm. The storm's winds and claps of thunder lead to the cleansing rain, and the peaceful stillness finally follows the powerful release.

Clearing and releasing in this way can also include a *fire ceremony* to dispose of the letter. Watching the letter go from paper, to flames, and then to ashes in a fireplace can be a great visual validation of the transformation process that you have just experienced. A paper shredder is another effective way to dispose of the Letter for Release after it has served its purpose.

JOURNALING:

Meditate for a few minutes and explore your history for "unfinished business" that would serve your highest good to process and release. Unfinished business* can include anger, hurts, losses, disappointments, fears, resentments...Here are some categories to explore:

- Relationships
- Health Issues
- Money
- Career

1. Write a letter about an issue that needs a voice—knowing you won't mail it. Using unbound paper is recommended so that you may dispose of your Letter for Release when you feel ready. If it is about a topic unrelated to a specific person, use your imagination as to what title to choose.

For example, if your Letter for Release is about money or financial challenges, then you could address this letter to the Director of Monetary Disbursements (yeah, it's okay to have a sense of humor here). Or start with, Dear Cosmic Financial Distributor.

2. Complete this sentence through journaling:

What's clear to me now is...

---

*If you begin processing some "unfinished business" that feels so highly charged that you experience an overwhelming amount of feelings, then simply stop this exercise and consider talking with a mental health professional.

Thoughts... Emotions... Memories... Sensations...

Inner Explorations and Inquiries...

Thoughts... Emotions... Memories... Sensations...

Inner Explorations and Inquiries...

Thoughts... Emotions... Memories... Sensations...

11

Mirror Letter

I have found this second step in the letter-writing process, the Mirror Letter, very helpful. After I have clarified and released my raw emotions around an issue through the previous letter-writing exercise, I then take a courageous and *l-o-n-g* look in the mirror in order to write another letter that explores *my* side of the street.

For example, if in my first letter I am processing a hurt I experienced with an ex-partner or friend, the Mirror Letter's purpose is to help me "own" my part of the dance. Relationship dances contain various actions and reactions from both partners, so I then look for my negative or hurtful behaviors in the dynamic. And keep in mind, for most of us, the first letters are *much* easier to write than these second ones!

Oftentimes, the Letter for Release is filled with blaming, self-righteous, holier-than-thou energy. The Mirror Letter, however, can be a humbling look at the challenges of our own behavior—the shadowy parts of us that take courage to face. If we are really brave, we will *connect-the-dots* and increase our understanding of *recurring life themes* or patterns.

"Oy vey," you may sigh and then ask, "Why does growth have to be *so-o-o* much work?" The reply would simply be that the more we integrate our shadowy parts by bringing them into our awareness, the more awake, whole, balanced, and authentic we become. Owning our issues also enables us to wake up and get our lessons. As a result, we won't be as likely to continuously sleepwalk and *repeat, repeat, repeat...*

JOURNALING:

1. Meditate for a few minutes about the Letter for Release that you wrote and explore whether you had some personal responsibility in the situation. If something comes to mind, write a Mirror Letter (that you *do not* plan to send) as a follow-up and address the person or entity you wrote in the first letter. Or, if it feels appropriate, address this letter to yourself.

Write directly in this journal or on a separate sheet of paper if you prefer.

2. Now that you have more clarity, think about whether there is someone you feel the need to have a *heart-to-heart talk* with. Take another few minutes to meditate on this topic. And, if writing a Letter of Amends to someone would bring no harm to you or anyone else, in any way, consider doing this for your own growth. (This can be an "extra credit" exercise.)

When I have written letters to make amends, I know that it is important to not be attached to the other person's response—since that is out of my realm of control. Rarely have I made amends and had the other person reciprocally own their negative behaviors in the dance. And that's okay; I chose to own and apologize in order to clean up *my* side of the street, not *theirs.* This process of *issue ownership* wakes me up. Consequently, I avoid repeating behaviors that do not serve my highest good. Then I get to enjoy the inner peace that often follows integrating a shadowy part of myself. Doing this makes looking in the mirror with more compassionate, *soft eyes* easier and easier.

3. Complete this sentence through journaling:

What's clear to me now is…

Thoughts... Emotions... Memories... Sensations...

Inner Explorations and Inquiries...

Thoughts... Emotions... Memories... Sensations...

Inner Explorations and Inquiries...

Thoughts... Emotions... Memories... Sensations...

12

Metamorphosis

Metamorphosis is a word that describes *changes in form.* In the insect world, this term is used to define the developmental stages of a butterfly. As most of us learned in grade school, an egg first develops into a caterpillar, and then the caterpillar spins a silk cocoon, or chrysalis around itself. When the chrysalis matures, a beautiful butterfly bursts forth from the cocoon.

In humans, *changes in form* are not always as consistent, predictable, or "as pretty" as they are in the insect world. They do, however, often make great stories—after we are on the other side of the change. Sometimes, to our chagrin, circumstances propel us into changes kicking and screaming. In these tough transitional times, our resistance is high because it feels like we are losing control.

Note three important words in the last sentence: *resistance* and *losing control.* Isn't a fear of losing control at the *core* of resisting change? "Will I be okay?" "What will happen next?" and "Will I survive?" can be common questions swirling in our minds when we are in the midst of change.

In my private practice, talking about change is a common occurrence. Although individual circumstances vary, there are similar threads. Seeing a client in the throes of change often prompts me to clarify that uncertainty, confusion, chaos, and disorientation are natural feelings during transitional times.

"Change is a metamorphic process," I explain. "We may outgrow a job, an unhealthy behavior, a relationship, or a negative core belief about ourselves. In the *interim stage* of transformation—the period between two events—it is natural to feel vulnerable and anxious. The truth is, this stage can be the hardest part of change. We have left the known and familiar—but we haven't reached our destination yet."

No matter how we frame it, change is challenging for many of us. And since dealing with change is an ongoing issue for all of us, let's see what inspiring lessons we can learn from Madame Butterfly.

Four Stages of the Metamorphosis Process

1. The Egg Stage

This stage represents a time of dormancy. We are in the dark without awareness or skills to know how to deal with something life has brought forth. We are probably whispering, "Who turned out the light?" Underdeveloped resources may be inside of us, but unfortunately, they are not within our reach yet. In the darkness of the Egg Stage, we often feel alone and scared.

We may retreat into an Egg Stage due to a loss or a traumatic event. As a result, we are thrown into a place of uncertainty. Hopefully, after incubating for a while, we will gather the resources needed to move forward. Sometimes this movement forward is the result of compassionate, loving help we will receive from others—or we courageously find a way to propel *ourselves* into the next stage.

By contrast, we may *invite* an Egg Stage into our lives, like when we decide to try something new. If we are starting from scratch, and we are not a child prodigy, then we will begin at the Egg Stage. Remember when we tried Salsa Dancing for the first time—and stepped on our partner's toes a lot? Yep, we were smack-dab in the middle of the Egg Stage again, wondering, "Who turned out the light?"

2. The Caterpillar Stage

In this stage, we are belly down and are continually taking in sustenance in order to survive. The fact is, caterpillars are known to eat voraciously and grow until they get too big for their *britches*—I mean skins. One type of moth caterpillar eats 86,000 times its birth weight during the first 56 days of its life. (Uh oh, maybe this is why some of us overeat when we're stressed! It's our *caterpillar survival instincts).* Meanwhile, when the caterpillar's skin becomes too tight, he sheds it and discovers the skin underneath. This shedding happens several times in preparation for the final transformation.

I have shed enough skins in my life to fill Cher's closet. Undoubtedly, some *shedding sessions* have been more graceful than others. When I have resisted change it has made the process especially tough. This *white-knuckling habit* has been riddled with rebellion and often resulted in backaches!

"But, hey," I would grumble, "Why let go of an identity without a fight?"

Yes, the deteriorated skin *was* uncomfortable, clearly outgrown, and had numerous splitting seams. Still, I held on for dear life—terrified of "the unknown" lurking beneath the worn-out, yet, familiar skin. Finally, after letting go, wriggling out, and moving forward, I discovered that the underlying new skin fit who I was in that moment. What a pleasant surprise!

A personal example of the Caterpillar Stage occurred when I outgrew my job as an Art Director designing "cutesy" products. I resisted change for years because I simply did not know where to go next. I only knew that the skin I was in *did not fit anymore.* I was quietly clinging to my outgrown identity, while avoiding moving forward into the unknown. During this stage, I voraciously devoured personal growth/psychology books. In addition, I attended many inspiring workshops and trainings—I was definitely *a woman on a mission!*

Finally, after repeatedly filling my belly with this Soul Food, I let the tattered skin *fall away* and nervously entered the next stage.

3. The Cocoon Stage

This stage happens when the caterpillar spins a chrysalis to rest in. During the cocoon period, unlike the previous stage of the voraciously hungry caterpillar, outside resources are not sought. This transformation is strictly an *internal process.*

My Cocoon Stages have used meditation as a vehicle to go within. When I am integrating challenging life lessons, my time in the cocoon allows me to be alone with my thoughts and feelings. This undistracted focus helps me *get to the heart* of what I need to learn. These treks inward have been incredibly rich, although sometimes painful. As a result, I often discover the *gifts* of my lessons.

When I had outgrown my Art Director identity, my Cocoon Stage allowed me to delve into the "Four W's." These important questions wanted to know—*who, what, when, and where?*

- *Who* am I today?
- *What* is my Life's purpose?

- *When* should I begin fulfilling it?
- *Where* do I go next to gather resources and appropriate mentors?

I explored these questions by repeatedly connecting to my Inner Consultant. After careful consideration, I created a practical map for myself. This map contained small steps that I could take to find resources and start moving toward creating personal growth products. It was a step-by-step model that I could follow to begin fulfilling my life's purpose of helping others. After receiving the gifts of this Cocoon Stage, with map in hand, I was ready to move forward again.

4. The Butterfly Stage

This stage only happens after substantial inner shifts and changes have taken place. The once earthbound caterpillar has become elongated and has magically sprouted wings. Ready for its final transformation, the fully-formed butterfly bursts from the safety of its cocoon, eager to fly. After spreading its wings and gliding around the garden, the butterfly begins to sip delicious nectar from the flowers. The period of isolation has ended. The butterfly reconnects to the outer world with expanded vision. It now has the ability to explore new horizons and experience a *higher vision.*

How many times in our lives have we experienced the beauty, grace, and *higher vision* of a butterfly's perspective? Some of us have had opportunities to spread and enjoy our beautiful wings, while others blocked their ability to do this. Maybe there was an unwillingness to let go, surrender, and trust that a greater force could move them through the various stages. Or perhaps a protective part of themselves knew that more inner strength and outer resources were needed before letting go and safely moving forward.

It is helpful to remember that each soul has its own divine timing for transformation. Metamorphosis can neither be *forced nor rushed.*

I feel as though my butterfly emerged from its Cocoon Stage when I became a Certified Clinical Hypnotherapist. My wings have felt further strengthened by writing this book. Sharing my voice through writing and teaching is one of the greatest gifts I have received thus far. When I first connected with my authentic voice, it felt as though the parts of my soul that were lost during a painful childhood returned home. So for this reason, having a voice in the world today feels truly amazing. Not only can I speak *my truth*—I also get to use my voice to *support* others. What a blessing!

I often refer to my hypnotherapy office as The Healing Cocoon. A drawing of a butterfly that I created 20 years ago hangs on the wall. This tiny, yet cozy, space has a skylight above the client's reclining chair. Each time a client experiences a personal transformation, I imagine that a beautiful butterfly is formed and symbolically set free through the skylight. It is an honor to hold the sacred space for the numerous transformations that have occurred in The Healing Cocoon.

And, transformation is not a "one-shot-deal." We are all required to repeatedly embrace the metamorphosis process throughout our life spans. One example of metamorphosis is the aging process. Aging not only affects our bodies, if we live long enough, it will also affect our careers. While we are still breathing, no part of our lives is standing completely still. We are all ever-changing *works in progress!*

For this reason, we may experience different metamorphic stages simultaneously in various areas of our lives. For instance, my client Joan was going through a challenging Egg Stage in her career. She felt alone, powerless, and in the dark about her work challenges. Yet, in her relationship with her husband she was experiencing great fulfillment and was therefore in a Butterfly Stage.

Accepting who we are, where we are, *and continually* seeking new tools and resources are signs that we are courageously living our lives. Humbly learning how to *fall in love with ourselves*, no matter which metamorphic stage of life we are in—is the sign of a seasoned and enlightened traveler.

JOURNALING:

1. Think of a past experience that was challenging. Here is a list of areas to explore:

- Relationships
- Health Issues
- Money
- Career
- Spirituality

2. Take a few minutes and review your past challenge through meditation. Journal about it by answering the following questions:

- What was the challenge?
- What inner and outer resources did you use to get through the challenge?
- If you look back on it from a *higher vision,* do you see any personal growth *gifts* you received from the experience?
- Can you identify any metamorphic stages you moved through to get to the other side?
    - The Egg Stage
    - The Caterpillar Stage
    - The Cocoon Stage
    - The Butterfly Stage

3. Are you currently going through a transition? If so, journal about it and explore whether you are in one of the metamorphic stages. What inner and outer resources can you connect with to support your transition?

4. Complete this sentence through journaling:

What's clear to me now is…

Thoughts… Emotions… Memories… Sensations…

Inner Explorations and Inquiries...

Thoughts… Emotions… Memories… Sensations…

Inner Explorations and Inquiries...

Thoughts... Emotions... Memories... Sensations...

13

Gratitude

Having an attitude-of-gratitude is a powerful state of mind and a great stress-busting tool. Whether we are naturally grateful or intentionally choose this attitude is not the issue. We benefit either way. This tool puts us in a win-win position. Feeling grateful for having shelter, food, clothes, money, and people that care about us are healthy gifts to our bodies, minds, and spirits.

On the other hand, it is common to over-focus on what's not right in our lives. When we feel nothing is ever good enough, we may habitually yearn for what we don't have. And, if an overly active Inner Critic is on board, we may add to the stressful pattern by having recurring thoughts like, "I'm not thin enough, smart enough, or hard-working enough."

For example, whenever something bothered me in the past my *worry cycle* would take over. My brain would feel like a hamster in an exercise wheel. As a kid, I had pet hamsters. These precious, nocturnal creatures raced in their squeaky wheels all night long. Similarly, when my worrying would become activated, it was running rampant in a squeaky wheel—*a stress wheel.* This racing got me nowhere and, unlike my hamsters, I did not burn one calorie in the process!

Thankfully, when I catch myself on an unproductive track these days, I pull out a stress-reducing tool. So, next time you find yourself in a worry cycle, think about whether there is some constructive action you can do. If something comes to mind, go for it. Also, consider doing research, getting advice, support, or whatever will help you get over and beyond the challenge. Taking action will hopefully get you out of the helpless mode and onto an empowered and productive track.

However, if you can't think of any positive action, then try the following:

Attitude-of-Gratitude Tool

For years, embracing an attitude-of-gratitude has been a highly recommended practice by numerous 12-Step programs. The reason is this: focusing on positive feelings, like gratitude, moves us out of the *victim role.* Furthermore, fear, anger, and sadness have difficulty coexisting with positive feelings, like gratitude. So, to hit the brakes on your *worry wheel,* try doing this simple three-step process:

1) Pull out a pen and a piece of paper or write directly in this journal.

2) Take a few abdominal breaths to get out of your head and to deepen your connection with your body.

3) Make a list of people, places, animals, and things for which you feel grateful. Yep, this may sound too simple, but give it a chance. If your brain resists shifting gears and nothing comes to mind, then start where you're standing. Are you wearing clothing? Do you have shoes on your feet? Great! Then these are your first things to write down. Is there a roof over your head? Good, you're both clothed and sheltered.

Once you get out of the hamster wheel, the positive juices will probably start flowing. Make your gratitude list and hopefully you will feel an emotional shift followed by a physical shift of *less tension* in your body. The goal of this tool is to assist you in moving from your head into your heart. Consider this attitude-of-gratitude as one simple way of going from north to south—*without ever having to get into your car.*

JOURNALING:

1. Gratitude can be a beautiful light we shine on ourselves. Which of your personality traits are you grateful for? Are you tenacious, hard working, sensitive, or compassionate? Now broaden the light of gratitude and list some people, places, or things in your life for which you feel grateful.

2. The attitude-of-gratitude is a great stress buster when you need to shift away from negativity. It is also a wonderful way to end each day and can serve as a sweet foundation for restful sleep. Before going to sleep, try the following writing exercises:

- Ask yourself, "What's Buggin' Me?" Write about whatever comes to mind (Chapter 4's Tool).
- Jot down five things you are grateful for.

3. Complete this sentence through journaling:

What's clear to me now is…

Inner Explorations and Inquiries...

Thoughts… Emotions… Memories… Sensations…

Inner Explorations and Inquiries…

Thoughts... Emotions... Memories... Sensations...

Inner Explorations and Inquiries...

Thoughts... Emotions... Memories... Sensations...

14

Victories!

This is the chapter that will serve as a container for your *many victories*, both small and large. If "tooting your own horn" makes you feel uncomfortable, then manage your anxiety by utilizing some of the stress reduction tools you have learned earlier in this journal. You have an opportunity here to practice being proud of *all your talents, skills, and unique personality qualities!*

And, please consider breaking-out-of-the-box when it comes to what society deems as positive accomplishments or victories. One great aspect of having gone to art school and worked in the publishing world with numerous "creative types," is my ability to treasure quirkiness. Let's face it, we creative souls are often "dancing" to a totally different drummer! And how refreshing is that?!

When I was a Design Director for a publisher in Northern California, my art department was filled with gems. Each artist was reliable, talented, and we managed to have more fun than any place I'd ever worked! Quirky and playful energy was rampant throughout the department. It was a priceless experience. This delightful "cast of characters" taught me how to treasure all sorts of personality types—and believe me—there was rarely a dull moment!

Keep in mind that positive thoughts and humor are both excellent stress busters. Are you ready to stretch your *positive capacity* by celebrating your personal victories every day? The following computer analogy will illustrate how important it is to stretch your positive capacity and thus increase your self-esteem. Think of your capacity to hold feelings as a computer hard drive. Most of us know that all hard drives have a limited amount of storage space. So, if your internal hard drive is filled with negative feelings about yourself, then there may be little room left for positive feelings or high self-esteem. By continually reporting your personal victories in this journal, you will be honoring "who you are," your value, and unique talents. Each victory list you create will send outdated or negative feelings about yourself into the computer's trash bin. *Yeah!*

You may find that you are squirming in your seat for the first few days while writing your victories. But, if you keep it up, chances are you will eventually get comfortable with this exercise. Remember that it takes twenty-one days to break a habit or pattern. So be patient with yourself. After you have moved past your resistance, you may be surprised to find yourself feeling excited and proud while listing your daily victories. Then—look out world—it will be time to "strut-your-stuff" and truly *own your light!*

JOURNALING:

1. At the end of the day, meditate for a few minutes and look for things you did that you feel good about. Acknowledge victories in various aspects of your life. For example: relationships, mental-physical-spiritual health, money, leisure, and career. Also, list victories that relate to your E.Q. or emotional intelligence, such as self-awareness, empathy, social skills, zeal, self-motivation, impulse control, and persistence. Don't hold back—let your lists get downright boisterous! Here is a sample:

Victories!

- I let in several compliments today without resistance; I simply remembered to breathe them in, smile, and say, "Thank you."
- I told my brother that I love and appreciate him.
- I mailed my tax forms on time.
- I managed my anxiety before and during my presentation.
- I resisted eating any candy at the office today!
- I prepared fresh vegetable snacks last night, and enjoyed nibbling them during break times.
- I took a walk with a colleague at lunch.
- I meditated this morning for 15 minutes. It felt great.

Remember to write victories that are both small and large. Also, throughout the day, when you accomplish something, give yourself internal compliments like, "Good job! Well done," and, "Hey that was gutsy!" This positive self-talk, in addition to writing your victories in your journal is a great way to build your self-esteem. By doing so, you will be developing your Inner Supporter or Cheerleader.

After meditating a few minutes to retrieve your accomplishments, it will be time for you to jot down some victories. Then, pucker those lips and get ready to "toot your own horn." *Ready—set—write!*

2. For a change of pace, later this week, you may want to list victories that you have accomplished so far this year. Or, make a list of the 10 victories you are most proud of that have happened throughout your life. This list ought to leave you smiling. Consider sharing it with your significant other or a close friend.

3. Complete this sentence through journaling:

What's clear to me now is...

Inner Explorations and Inquiries...

Thoughts... Emotions... Memories... Sensations...

Inner Explorations and Inquiries...

Thoughts... Emotions... Memories... Sensations...

Inner Explorations and Inquiries...

Thoughts... Emotions... Memories... Sensations...

15

Synthesis

Here you are, ready to embrace the last chapter. If you have worked with each exercise, then you have refined and polished various facets of yourself. Like the facets of the *gem* featured on this book cover, your ability to reflect more of your *Inner Light* depends on how *synthesized* you feel from the inside out.

Now that you have explored different aspects of your mind-body-spirit through the exercises of this book, do you feel a deeper connection to yourself as a result? If so, then do you also sense that you're being more authentic in your life? Authenticity is about being real. It is about owning your *power* as well as your *vulnerability.* I often tell my clients that getting stuck in one or the other is a trap. Honoring polar opposites synthesizes the soul. For example, knowing how to *hold both your joys and your sorrows* is a courageous achievement. Having a connection to your Inner Critic as well as your Inner Supporter/Cheerleader is another example of internal balancing.

However, to honor and balance your emotions you must first have access to them. For instance, being aware of your feelings and therefore knowing, "What's buggin' me?" is just as important as feeling gratitude, and owning your daily victories. Having access to your Inner Consultant is another wonderful ability that helps to create more inner balance and reduce stress. Emotional synthesis is a valuable skill that allows you to *honor and hold it all.*

Breathing is also a great stress reducer. As you learned earlier, over-breathing or breath holding can be an invitation for a Stress Response. Tools you have worked with throughout this book focused on increasing your ability to turn Stress Responses into Relaxation Responses through various mind-body approaches. You did exercises to heighten your Emotional Intelligence

(E.Q.), communication skills, behavioral health, intuition, and abilities to manage transitions and change.

And hopefully, you read my favorite chapter, *Soft Eyes.* Seeing yourself lovingly, through soft eyes is an amazing gift to your soul. A combination of compassion and self-love is a priceless foundation to build your life on. Undoubtedly, your stress levels will drop dramatically when you love yourself enough to honor your feelings and needs each and every day.

Congratulations for finishing this journal! I am leaving you with some suggestions for Maintenance and Tools to Use as Needed. I wish you the best as you continue to move along the path of learning to *stress less* and *love more.*

—Suggestions for Maintenance—

Morning Meditation Practice

Beginner's Simple Meditation: (from the Introduction)

Spend ten to twenty minutes meditating.

Evening Journaling Practice

Buy a blank journal and place four tabs to divide the journal into four parts. The tab suggestions are as follows:

Tab 1: What's Buggin' Me? (from Chapter 4)
Under this first tab, get anything that is bothering you off your chest. Remember to scan for bodily tension and write about that too.

Tab 2: Inner Consultant Wisdom (from Chapter 3)
Meditate for a moment or two and connect with your Inner Consultant (or whatever you have named your Higher Self). Then, under this second tab, give your Inner Consultant a voice by journaling its responses to whatever you wrote under the first tab about what is bothering you. To self-soothe, you can also dialogue back and forth with the part of you that is stressed. Use your Active Listening skills (Chapter 5): mirroring, validation, and empathy. You will be surprised how effective these tools are to lower stress!

Tab 3: Attitude-of-Gratitude (from Chapter 13)
Under this third tab, list five or more things that you feel grateful for. Remember to look *inside* yourself as well as *outside* yourself.

Tab 4: Victories (from Chapter 14)
Under this fourth tab, jot down some of your victories from the day. Strut your stuff!

Spend ten or more minutes journaling before sleeping.
Sweet dreams...

—Tools to Use as Needed—	
When You Feel	**You Can Do the Exercises From**
Stressed or anxious	Chapter 1: Tiger Taming Chapter 2: Coming Home
Anger, sadness, or disappointment	Chapter 4: What's Buggin' Me? Chapter 10: Letter for Release
Unfulfilled or empty	Chapter 8: Soul Nourishment
When You Have	**You Can Do the Exercises From**
Relationship challenges	Chapter 5: The Art of Listening Chapter 6: Oops, Triangulation Chapter 10: Letter for Release Chapter 11: Mirror Letter
Inner Critic attacks	Chapter 4: What's Buggin' Me? Chapter 7: Soft Eyes Chapter 13: Gratitude
Unhealthy habits	Chapter 9: Undesirable Urges
Transition & change	Chapter 12: Metamorphosis
When You Want	**You Can Do the Exercises From**
Inner guidance	Chapter 3: Inner Wisdom

Thoughts... Emotions... Memories... Sensations...

Inner Explorations and Inquiries...

Thoughts... Emotions... Memories... Sensations...

Inner Explorations and Inquiries...

Thoughts... Emotions... Memories... Sensations...

Bibliography

American Psychiatric Association: *Diagnostic and Statistical Manual of Mental Disorders,* Fourth Edition, Text Revision. Washington, DC, American Psychiatric Association, 2000.

Bhat, N. (2002). *Reversing Stress and Burnout.* Concord, CA: Cybernetix Publishing.

Davich, V. (1998). *The Best Guide to Meditation.* Los Angeles: Renaissance Books.

Goleman, D. (1995). *Emotional Intelligence.* New York: Bantam Books.

Gray, J. (1984). *What You Feel, You Can Heal.* Mill Valley, CA: Heart Publishing Company.

Rossman, M. (2000). *Guided Imagery for Self-Healing.* Tiburon, CA: HJ Kramer, and Novato, CA: New World Library.

Stein, J. (2003, August 4). The Science of Meditation. *Time,* 48-56.

Stone, H., and S. Stone. (1989). *Embracing Our Selves.* Novato, CA: New World Library.

About the Author

Trina Swerdlow, B.F.A., C.C.H.T., is a certified clinical hypnotherapist, an author, an artist, and an ordained minister. Trina received her hypnotherapy credential from HCH Institute in Lafayette, California. She is also a meditation teacher with over twenty-five years of personal meditation experience.

Her artwork appears in seven books, on hundreds of greeting cards, and on numerous other gift products. Trina received her B.F.A. (Bachelor in Fine Art) from Art Center College of Design in Pasadena, California. Her illustrations and profile are included in *Outstanding American Illustrators Today 2.* She wrote and illustrated the personal growth book, *Growing Free.* In addition, Trina created the Thera-Tool Figure, a therapeutic gestalt product endorsed by bestselling author, John Gray. Counselors across the U.S. use the Thera-Tool Figure in their clinical work. In 2002, author Naras Bhat, M.D., F.A.C.P., and Trina completed *Reversing Stress and Burnout.* She was the book's creative director, cover designer, editor, and illustrator. Included in Dr. Bhat's book is Trina's own method for countering anxiety.

Trina has a private practice in Danville, California, where she offers stress management tools that include meditation and journaling instruction. She also teaches various stress management classes at The Women's Health Center of the John Muir/Mt. Diablo Health System in Walnut Creek, California. Her hypnotherapy training, meditation experience, art, and writing come together as the transformational tools that Trina soulfully shares with her clients today.

978-0-595-37455-7
0-595-37455-7

Printed in the United States
41110LVS00004B/292-390

9 780595 374557